Research shows that five strategies are associated with the successful completion of a dissertation:

- Establishing a consistent writing routine
- Working with a support group
- Consulting your adviser
- Understanding your committee's expectations
- Setting a realistic and timely schedule

Building on these insights, this book is for anyone who needs help in preparing for, organizing, planning, scheduling, and writing the longest sustained writing project they have encountered, particularly if he or she is not receiving sufficient guidance about the process, but also for anyone looking to boost his or her writing productivity.

The author uncovers much tacit knowledge, provides advice on working with dissertation advisers and committee members, presents proven techniques for the prewriting and writing stages of the dissertation, sets out a system for staying on schedule, and advocates enlisting peer support.

As Peg Boyle Single states, "My goal is quite simple and straightforward: for you to experience greater efficiency and enjoyment while writing. If you experience anxiety, blocking, impatience, perfectionism or procrastination when you write, then this system is for you. I want you to be able to complete your writing so that you can move on with the rest of your life."

Few scholars, let alone graduate students, have been taught habits of writing fluency and productivity. The writing skills imparted by this book will not only help the reader through the dissertation writing process, but will also serve her or him in whatever career she or he embarks on, given the paramount importance of written communication, especially in the academy.

This book presents a system of straightforward and proven techniques that are used by productive writers and applies them to the dissertation process. In particular, it promotes the concept of writing networks—whether writing partners or groups—to ensure that writing does not become an isolated and tortured process, while not masking the need for persistence and sustained effort.

This book is intended for graduate students and their advisers in the social sciences, the humanities, and professional fields. It can further serve as a textbook for either informal writing groups led by students or for formal writing seminars offered by departments or graduate colleges. The techniques described will help new faculty advise their students more effectively and even achieve greater fluency in their own writing.

Praise from the Author's Workshop Participants

"Dr. Single's book should be must reading for graduate students and researchers seeking to efficiently and strategically read and synthesize scholarly articles. Peg's methods helped me tremendously as I completed my Ph.D. in Natural Resource Planning. Her strategic technique helped me make the best use of my time. I continue today to use the writer's notes and methods I developed under Peg's guidance. This book will be invaluable to anyone pursuing a graduate degree. I highly recommend it."

—**Richard Watts**, Ph.D. in Natural Resource Planning
from the University of Vermont

"Dr. Single's book is not only useful for those working toward completion of the dissertation, but also for individuals taking on any long-term writing project. I have used elements of this book to complete my own dissertation and continue to draw upon its wisdom currently as a tenure track faculty member."

—**Dannielle Joy Davis**, Ph.D. in Educational Policy Studies
from the University of Illinois at Urbana-Champaign

"Dr. Single's techniques provide the foundation that will allow you complete your research and writing. Daily writing, even for short periods of time, is the key to success."

—**Karen F. Madden**, Ph.D. in American History
from Michigan State University

"The Single System provided me with the courage to write by giving me the skills and techniques that made the dissertation much more manageable. The interactive notes, citeable notes, and interactive reading exercises moved me from a point of fear and writer's block towards a pattern of writing fluency. Having learned these useful techniques as a doctoral student, I now teach them to my own students, who appreciate knowing the social and cultural forces that influence their ability to write and techniques that assist them in overcoming these obstacles. Dr. Single's System substantively contributed to my ability to narrow my focus, begin the writing process, and, most importantly, craft a dissertation of which I could be proud."

—**Alvin Sturdivant**, Ed.D. in Educational Leadership and
Policy Studies from the University of Vermont

"I highly recommend Dr. Single's book. She presents a writing system that helps you progress from unformed idea to finished product in a manner that suits your style and brings out the best in your scholarship and your writing."

—**Anne Chan**, Ph.D. in Counseling Psychology
from Stanford University

"*Demystifying Dissertation Writing* provides clear and comprehensive direction for graduate students in any discipline. Dr. Single's practical, step-by-step guidelines not only helped me finish my dissertation in sociology, but her specific techniques transformed my approach to writing. Her system truly demystifies the process and makes the dissertation writing experience manageable and even enjoyable. I highly recommend this book—it is packed with helpful tips and effective strategies designed to help doctoral students succeed."

—**Kimberly Huisman**, Ph.D. in Sociology
from the University of Southern California

"Writing a dissertation is one of the most difficult and painful tasks of one's academic career. Fortunately for us, Dr. Single has mastered and found a way to synthesize this process into a step-by-step guidebook that, as its title suggests, demystifies dissertation writing. I found it to be an invaluable tool during my dissertation journey, and it is a must-have for any doctoral student wishing not just to survive, but to thrive during this process."

—**Stacey A. Miller**, Ed.D. in Educational Leadership and
Policy Studies from the University of Vermont

DEMYSTIFYING DISSERTATION WRITING

A *Streamlined* Process from Choice of Topic to Final Text

Peg Boyle Single, Ph.D.

Foreword by Richard M. Reis, Ph.D.

STERLING, VIRGINIA

COPYRIGHT © 2010 BY PEG BOYLE SINGLE.

Published by Stylus Publishing, LLC
22883 Quicksilver Drive
Sterling, Virginia 20166-2102

Library of Congress Cataloging-in-Publication-Data
Single, Peg Boyle, 1963–
    Demystifying dissertation writing : a streamlined process from choice of topic to final text / Peg Boyle Single.
        p.   cm.
    Includes bibliographical references and index.
    ISBN 978-1-57922-312-0 (cloth : alk. paper)
    ISBN 978-1-57922-313-7 (pbk. : alk. paper)
1. Dissertations, Academic—Authorship.   2. Academic writing.   I. Title.
LB2369.55   2010
808′.02—dc22

                                                    2009026742

13-digit ISBN: 978-1-57922-312-0 (cloth)
13-digit ISBN: 978-1-57922-313-7 (paper)

Printed in the United States of America

All first editions printed on acid free paper that meets the American National Standards Institute Z39-48 Standard.

Bulk Purchases

Quantity discounts are available for use in workshops and for staff development.
Call 1-800-232-0223

First Edition, 2009

10   9   8   7   6   5   4   3

To Rich

You bring so much love, joy, happiness, and meaning to my life, without you this book would never have been written.

And to Robert Boice,

my dissertation adviser and mentor.

CONTENTS

ACKNOWLEDGMENTS

TO SAY THAT THIS BOOK was built on the shoulders of those who went before me is an understatement. I would like to offer my appreciation and thanks to Bob Boice for introducing me to his method for fluent writing and for taking a chance on me. Much of what I present in these pages is a derivation of what I learned from him. He is an amazingly warm and generous man who has helped many writers through the books he has written on writing and through advice to new faculty. His many bits of wisdom about writing and life I carry with me.

I have so many people to thank who have helped me along the way. Thanks to Christa Vetter, who helped me get started on the journey to graduate school, literally and metaphorically, as she drove with me cross-country from California to New York. Thanks to David Boedy for helping make a dream a reality. Thanks to Julie Exline for being my writing partner since we were in graduate school. Many times I thought I would never write again, and perhaps would not have, without Jules's support and wisdom.

Special thanks to Pablo Bose, Randall Harp, Susan Hasazi, Karen Madden, JoAnn Moody, Robert J. Nash, Megan Ohler, Jane Okech, Tim Prevo, and Elisa Ziglar for their encouragement and/or feedback on earlier drafts of this book. Thank you to all the students who have taken my writing seminar, whose candidness and experience provided me with unique insights into the writing process. I also greatly appreciate the support of my writing group, who provided invaluable advice and support while I was finding a publisher and completing this book (Clare Ginger, Kathy Manning, and Denise Youngblood).

I am grateful to John von Knorring of Stylus Publishing for his support and encouragement. I also want to thank the three anonymous reviewers who read an early version of *Demystifying Dissertation Writing*. This book is better because of your helpful and candid comments.

Thanks to Frank and Dotty Boyle (Mom and Dad, to me). They have provided unwavering love and support and have expressed the utmost confidence in me in all my endeavors. Thanks to Theresa Boyle for her love and support and for visiting with Aydan and Liam for regular fun-filled breaks from writing. To Donna Fontana, many thanks for being the best lifelong friend anyone could have hoped for—you are an inspiration to me. Your ability to balance a successful career with international travel, your impressive capacity for maintaining close friendships, and your involvement in community service continue to inspire me.

My greatest appreciation goes to the two with whom I share my home. My dog, Felix, was my writing companion while I was working on this book. He kept me company by sleeping underneath my desk while I sat at the computer. Richard is my husband and the love of my life. Before I met him I could never have imagined being so happy and enjoying life so much. This book could never have been written without his love, support, and laughter.

PREFACE

OR MORE THAN FIFTEEN YEARS I have conducted writing seminars and provided writing coaching to graduate students and new
faculty members. During this time, I have helped doctoral students
complete dissertations who otherwise would be at risk for remaining ABD
(all-but-dissertation). I have seen new faculty members engage in a writing program that all but ensured their earning tenure. In all cases, I have
worked with academic writers who are bright, motivated, creative, and
interesting. They learn quickly. When they come to me for help with
writing I can be sure of one thing: They have never been taught habits of
writing fluency and productivity.

Rarely do they discuss their writing concerns with colleagues or classmates. Because writing is a hallmark of success in academe, admitting
such weaknesses would open them to concerns of "not having what it
takes." As a result, too many struggle in isolation, not only at the expense
of their writing, but also at the expense of their health or personal life.

When I meet writers who do admit their difficulties with writing, they
are reassured when I tell them that they are not alone. They are also
surprised at how a little coaching can go a long way. Learning habits of
fluent writing can be short on effort and long on effect, especially for
those who have a record of excelling at learning. I know because I have
watched more than a hundred academics dramatically improve their writing fluency and scholarly productivity. I know because I used to be a
blocked writer. Techniques of fluent writing, techniques used by productive writers, can be taught and learned and are readily transferable to you.

If you are a doctoral student who wants to improve your writing or a
faculty member or administrator who wants to support your doctoral

students as they complete their dissertations, this book can help. I wrote this book for graduate students and their advisers in the social sciences, the humanities, and professional fields. This book can serve as a textbook for informal writing groups led by students or formal writing seminars offered by departments or graduate colleges.

My goal in writing this book is to disseminate writing techniques so that as many graduate students as wish could learn these techniques. I do, however, also hold a loftier goal: to demystify the writing process (thus the title of this book). I am concerned with this demystification because of my commitment to democratizing the academy. My reasons for linking writing to democratizing the academy are fourfold.

First, writing continues to be the hallmark of intelligence in our society. Although there are notable exceptions (often in the field of politics, social activism, and film), many who receive MacArthur Fellow genius awards, Nobel Prize awards, and Fields Medals and those who are interviewed by Terry Gross ultimately proved their expertise through some sort of writing.

The importance of writing is particularly evident in higher education, often referred to as the academy. To enter the academy, one has to write. To stay in the academy, one has to write. The notable exception is at community colleges, where the focus is on teaching and advising.

The second reason I want to demystify the writing process is because writing is cloaked in mystique, allied with muses, and associated with myths, such as the myth of the isolated and tortured writer. Sure, plenty of successful writers fit the stereotype of the isolated and tortured writer—I just never wanted to be one of them. I want to write and live a happy and connected life. Do not misunderstand me: I wrote this book through many long hours sitting at my computer, nearly alone, save the companionship of my dog. But I was neither isolated nor tortured.

What I have found is that successful writers (at least the writers I want to emulate) inevitably have strong writing networks. These writers have writing partners or groups with whom they share early and embarrassingly error-prone drafts. I have yet to meet a writer who, when asked, does not have a network or support system of other writers.

Although I freely debunk the myth of the isolated and tortured writer, I want to underscore that writing is hard work. Fluent writers regularly work at writing. If the mystique of writing is shattered, it is by crashing through your internal barriers. If the myths are debunked, it is through persistent and sustained effort. If the writing muse ever appears, it is because she was coaxed, pleaded with, and pulled down from the heavens through regular sustained effort.

The third reason I seek to demystify the writing process is that writing still stratifies our society. Meanwhile, writing techniques are too rarely taught in formal settings. In graduate school, I found myself hanging out with other first-generation college students (we did not realize this common attribute while we were bonding). All three of us had learned our writing through the old Thorndike method of trial and error and had been successful with the semester-long papers we needed to complete. None of us had ever been taught how to write a lengthy academic paper. Although many of our classmates were not working class and a few had professors as parents, even they had not been taught the skills necessary to complete a dissertation in a timely manner.

I took two years of coursework during graduate school. It seemed necessary for me to take courses in which I would learn about psychological theories and experiments and study complex statistical analyses. Not once did my professors walk me through writing a long dissertation-length paper. There were no courses or training sessions on how to complete the one big project that separated me from earning my Ph.D. This was, and still is, untenable to me.

Mind you, this was no particular fault of my graduate program. At the time I was in graduate school, few psychology programs offered dissertation writing programs. Now more writing seminars are offered. Colleges of education seem to be on the forefront of offering structured support during the dissertation stage. I hope that this book supports doctoral students, whether they have access to formal dissertation writing seminars or not, to improve their writing process, increase the efficiency with which they finish their dissertation, and enjoy the process a little bit more.

Faculty members may not offer writing seminars because they may not think that their students need one. For instance, I was having lunch with another faculty member who was in the social sciences but not in my department. I told her about my dissertation writing seminar. Without giving it too much thought, she said, "My students don't need that." I had to chuckle when I heard the opposite response from two students in her department. One student was admittedly average; the other was known as a star. When my dissertation writing seminar came up in conversation, they wanted to hear more. They wished that their department offered a dissertation writing seminar for them and their classmates. Because of the selection bias and weeding out that occurs at the faculty ranks, faculty members may not think that offering a writing seminar is necessary for their students. Although by sponsoring these types of professional development opportunities, universities could increase the percentage of students who earn their doctoral degrees and widen the gates in terms of those who complete their degrees.

The previously stated reasons for my writing this book, that is, disseminating writing techniques to demystify the writing process, can be subsumed under one overarching goal. I wish to do my part in eroding the social Darwinism that pervades our educational systems. The survival of the fittest is evident beginning in kindergarten classrooms and continuing through to doctoral seminars. The skills and tools, or practical intelligence, necessary for success are rarely taught or made explicit. The implications are that the social class structure is reinforced so that the fluidity among class strata, which Americans hold as a central tenet of our meritocracy, is not fluid enough. Robert Sternberg, a leading psychological and educational researcher, discusses this in "Practical Intelligence for Success in School":

> Teachers have a wide array of expectations for students, many of which are never explicitly verbalized. Students who cannot meet these implicit expectations may suffer through year after year of poor school performance without knowing quite what is wrong. Their teachers expect them to know how to allocate their time in doing homework, how to prepare course papers, how to study for tests, how to talk (and not to talk) to a teacher—if they never learn these things, they will suffer for it.[1]

As a result of these beliefs that I hold dear, you will find that this book not only provides tips and techniques for prewriting and writing, it also supplies tips about practical intelligence and tacit knowledge. For instance, I offer suggestions for managing your dissertation adviser and committee members.

My fourth and final goal is quite simple and straightforward: for you to experience greater efficiency and enjoyment while writing. If you experience anxiety, blocking, impatience, perfectionism, or procrastination when you write, the Single System is for you. I want you to be able to complete your writing so that you can move on with the rest of your life. I want you to experience happiness while writing. I would never have thought it possible, but writing makes me happy. I manage my time and output so that it is reasonable. I modify my unrealistically high expectations. After I have completed my scheduled writing time (which is restricted because of my other personal and professional responsibilities), I can tackle the many other tasks I have to accomplish before the day is over.

Note

1. Robert J. Sternberg, Lynn Okagaki, and Alice S. Jackson, "Practical Intelligence for Success in School," 35.

FOREWORD

S INGLE SAYS that your dissertation should be the worst piece of research you ever write: not that it should be bad, but because all the scholarly writing you do after that should be even better. I agree, and that's why I'm so pleased that, even after forty years in higher education and a lifetime of professional writing, I found this book. I expect to use the advice in it for years to come. Although it is explicitly intended for doctoral students and their dissertation advisers in the social sciences and humanities, all academics at any stage of their career can benefit tremendously from it.

Its warm yet substantive style, with plenty of pithy quotes and lots of specific examples gleaned from years of working with doctoral students, makes the reading enjoyable as well as very practical.

The author spends almost the first half of the book talking about "pre-writing," which is what you do before you are ready to actually start writing your dissertation. By "ready" she doesn't mean "when you feel like it," but rather after you have done sufficient research, thinking, and interactive note taking that you don't go down the wrong path and end up throwing away much of what you will write.

Indeed, the advice on interactive reading and note taking is quite insightful and will save you a lot of time when you start to actually write your dissertation. It also provides a way of preparing for something that will be very important when you start looking for an academic position. Taking notes and, in the process, cataloging the contributions of the authors whose work you are reading is a great way to identify researcher colleagues for future contacts and interactions. Drop a note to the ones whose work you find particularly interesting and useful. If they respond, you have the opportunity to continue the dialogue with them directly. Having such contacts will be crucial when you enter the job market. Those contacts can help clear the pathway for your application to be considered, say something about your work, and suggest other institutions to which you might apply.

Single goes on to talk in depth about the importance of finding the right dissertation adviser and developing a dissertation topic. As she notes, "choosing a dissertation adviser will be the most important decision you make as a doctoral student." She also acknowledges that you may need to develop relationships with mentors and advisers other than your primary adviser. I agree: no one person, no matter how "right," can meet all your needs. You need to look for complementary advisers who can fill in what your major adviser can't provide. For example, if your major adviser is relatively young and inexperienced in supervising doctoral students but makes up for it in enthusiasm and the desire to establish a record of completed doctoral students, look for a complementary older adviser who is respected in the department and who has the wisdom to know what is really important to completing a doctorate and what can wait for a later time.

Another example of the broad usefulness of this book is in the discussion of focus statements. Such statements are one to four sentences that summarize and presage your entire dissertation. It can take weeks or even months to prepare these statements, after which you should memorize them. Such statements, and the ones you will develop in the future about your research, are also called "elevator talks," the answer you give to the what-are-you-working-on question posed by an inquiring party during the time it takes you to get from the first to the sixth floor in a fast elevator. Trust me, there are times when just such a situation will occur, particularly at conferences, and you will want to say something so interesting and compelling that the other person gets off the elevator with you and wants to hear your "hallway talk."

The book then goes on to describe in considerable detail the development of your one-page outline and then your much more detailed long outline, and it provides plenty of examples, all designed to set you up for the writing of your first draft. To accomplish that task, you need to develop a regular writing routine, and Single devotes a detailed chapter to showing you how to do so.

Single points out that the first draft is always the most difficult, and that revising is not as difficult cognitively, although it may be more time consuming. In other words, you need to get words and sentences—any words and sentences—on a screen so you can go back later and make revisions. While I was writing my book—a book of advice for doctoral students and new faculty members in scientific, technical, and mathematical fields—I found it useful to start with what is called *blind writing*. Set your word processor to numbering (that is, create a numbered list) and then turn down the brightness on the screen so that you can't see anything. Now start typing your thoughts, any thoughts, and when you finish a particular thought—at most a sentence or two—hit return and go on. Obviously you will not be able to worry about spelling or punctuation, and that is the whole point. No one but you will ever see this first effort. I found I could do this for only fifteen to twenty minutes at a time. But when I had finished, I had transferred my rambling thoughts into a first crude, post-outline draft, with specific points numbered for future reference. It may well have taken me twice or three times as long to edit this blind typing into something I would be willing to show someone, but it got me over the most difficult hump of getting started and led to my book *Tomorrow's Professor: Preparing for Academic Careers in Science and Engineering*.

Once you are ready to start doing this kind of writing, you need to commit to it on a regular, if limited, time per day basis. Forget about whether you feel motivated or not. As the novelist Peter De Vries noted, "I write when I'm inspired, and I see to it that I'm inspired at nine o'clock every morning."

Regular writing is the urgent and important activity you must do regularly and, if possible, before anything else in the day. It will give you a feeling of accomplishment that you will certainly need. In addition, as I have suggested to the dozens of new engineering faculty members who have attended the New Century Scholars workshops, make sure you are "establishing your absence." By that I mean finding a place, or places—preferably without Wi-Fi access—where you can hide out and write. For some people this can be a public place such as a restaurant or coffee house where they are essentially anonymous. For others it may have to be more quiet and isolated. The good news is that, with your laptop, you are as portable as you want and need to be.

Dr. Single concludes her excellent book with a discussion of how to approach revisions and how to have them reviewed by your dissertation committee members. Throughout her book, Single provides tips on managing your adviser and your committee members. Along those lines, one thing to consider when showing drafts of your chapters to your advisers is whether to send the same draft to all advisers at one time, in parallel, or one at a time, serially, with the comments of the previous reviewers attached. There is always a strong tendency for a reviewer to offer detailed comments, in part to show that they are holding up their end of the advising commitment. The advantage in the serial approach is that each subsequent reviewer can see what their colleagues have said and in many cases tell themselves, or just write in the margin, "I agree." It also makes them think twice about giving you contradictory advice. It takes longer and may sound somewhat manipulative, but it really is just another way to manage your committee.

So begin reading and benefiting from this book. I predict that you will continue, as I will, to do so for many years to come.

Richard M. Reis, Ph.D.
Editor of *Tomorrow's Professor eNewsletter*
Desktop Faculty Development, One Hundred Times a Year

Executive Director of the Alliance for Innovative Manufacturing (AIM) at Stanford and Co-Executive Director of the Stanford Research Communication Program

1

THE SINGLE SYSTEM FOR ACADEMIC WRITING

Blocking occurs when writers write before they are ready.

—Peg Boyle Single

I HAVE FAR TOO many writing memories that I would like to forget. I used to have a hard time sitting down to write. And when I did, I too often stared at a blank computer screen. To compensate for procrastinating, I had a history of pulling all-nighters to finish writing assignments. I rarely left myself the time for adequate revision. Nonetheless, I earned decent grades on these papers. But when it came to writing my dissertation, I feared that, despite my hard work throughout graduate school, I was at risk for being ABD (all-but-dissertation) because I struggled with writing.

Believe it or not (and I know some of you will believe it), I would rather have cleaned my kitchen floor than sit down in front of my computer to write my dissertation. Cleaning the kitchen floor had a few attractive elements as a procrastination task: It took a relatively short time to complete, it needed to be done regularly (especially with a dog who did not wipe his paws), and I could see results right away. While perfecting my procrastinating, at least I tried to engage in useful tasks.

Although I can now joke about my writer's block and self-sabotaging habits, when I was working on my dissertation they created serious problems for me. I had to develop new work and writing habits before I could finish a quality dissertation within a reasonable amount of time. Prior to working on my dissertation, my study and writing habits served me well. I had learned to study successfully for tests. I handed in coursework on time. I managed to write acceptable papers in my courses, even when pulling all-nighters to finish them. My work and study habits helped me get accepted into a doctoral program, complete the coursework, and pass the comprehensive and qualifying exams.

When I started working on my dissertation, the rules changed. The naturally occurring supports that helped me through two grueling years of coursework were removed. I was conducting my own research project without any externally imposed deadlines. Writing assignments for courses, although of considerable length, were much shorter than what was expected for my dissertation. Now the expectation was to write the longest and most complex piece of research and writing I had ever attempted, but with little training or direction regarding writing.

If I was to be successful in completing my doctoral dissertation, I realized that I had to learn new work habits, habits that would overcome the writer's block I imposed on myself. Well, I did learn new habits, thanks to a patient, wise, and supportive dissertation adviser. I was lucky that Robert (Bob) Boice, an expert on faculty development and writing fluency, was affiliated with my department and was willing to advise one last graduate student. Along with agreeing to be my dissertation adviser, he facilitated a writing group for several graduate students in my department. Not all of my classmates struggled with writing to the same extent that I did. Nonetheless, they knew a good thing when they saw it and were smart enough to admit that they could benefit greatly from attending a writing group.

Through the process of developing fluent writing habits, I realized that I had never been taught how to organize, plan, schedule, and execute a long-term, large-scale project the size of a dissertation. I also realized that if I had been taught these writing techniques earlier in my academic career, I would have saved myself from experiencing a lot of misery. Well, I hope to save you from experiencing some of this misery. Even if you do not experience misery while writing, I hope I am able to pass along a few writing tips that you find useful.

If you are reading this book, chances are you fall into one of the following categories:

- You have struggled with writing and writer's block throughout your graduate education and it has negatively affected your academic performance and personal well-being.
- You used to be a comfortable and fluent writer, but the enormity of your dissertation has triggered writer's block and avoidance.
- You are a comfortable and fluent writer who is constantly looking for ways to improve your productivity.
- You are an administrator or a faculty member of a doctoral program who has seen too many students struggle through the dissertation phase and you want to provide a structured way to support them.

If you are someone who struggles with writing, you will improve your writing by trying some of the techniques I propose in this book. If you are a comfortable and productive writer, you will find tips to improve your writing, tips that I learned from the many fluent writers I have met and whose books I have read. If you are a faculty member who facilitates or who plans to facilitate a writing seminar for your students, you can use this book as a textbook for your course.

Like all writing books, this one is not for everyone. You may have entered graduate school with strong training in planning and writing a large-scale writing project. As such, you may not find the advice on writing techniques and habits all that useful. Nevertheless, I think you will find the information about running a writing group useful.

Although many of the writing techniques that I present are universal and span academic disciplines, I focus this book on writing dissertations for the humanities and social sciences. I choose this focus because I have taught these writing techniques to social science and humanities graduate students in my courses and as a writing coach. In *Demystifying Dissertation Writing*, I coach you so that you will learn new writing techniques and habits. Whether you are pursuing a Ph.D., an Ed.D., a DrPH, a Psych.D., or any other doctoral degree, I do not want writing to come between you and earning your degree. Throughout this book, I reference research about the doctoral process, provide advice on choosing advisers, and suggest pointers on keeping your dissertation committee members happy. But mostly I demystify the academic writing process and show you that you have what it takes to finish a high-quality dissertation in a timely manner.

1.1. Developing Habits of Fluent Writing

You might notice that I focus on writing habits, not on writing skills. By the time you are accepted into a doctoral program, you pretty much have a handle on grammar, sentence structure, and word usage. Although you may not always comply with the rules of writing in English, you can spot mistakes, and given enough time, correct them in your own writing. The problem is that too often doctoral students are not taught habits of fluent writing, so their writing product is not aligned with their writing skills. Only through developing habits of fluent writing, engaging in effective prewriting, writing a pretty lousy first draft, and giving yourself enough time for revision will you live up to your writing potential.

A basic premise of developing habits of fluent writing is that you work in regular, moderate sessions. In spite of this, a common myth is that writing can be done effectively only in large blocks of time. I quickly and regularly debunk that myth. Fluent writers, especially those for whom writing is their primary career, write regularly and almost daily whether or not they have large blocks of free time. Also, I debunk the myth that inspiration drives the writing process. Although inspiration does play a large part in crystallizing the main focus of your dissertation, inspiration will not get you a completed dissertation.

In this book, I focus on the writing process, not on the knowledge generation process. What I mean by *knowledge generation process* is the process by which students in philosophy develop and defend an argument, students in English analyze texts, or students in economics analyze data. The scope of knowledge generation is broad, encompassing numerous theoretical/conceptual approaches to analysis, research methodologies, discursive methods, and methods of synthesis. The scope is too broad to include in this book, so I leave you to learn those techniques from your courses or other books. Just know that when I am referring to the various theoretical approaches to analysis and research methodologies, I will use the shortened term *theories and methods*.

1.2. Using *Demystifying Dissertation Writing* as a Guide for Writing Groups and Seminars

In this book, I present a system for academic writing as well as a framework for conducting an informal dissertation writing group or teaching a dissertation writing seminar. Although writing is a lone experience, writing does not have to be, nor should it be, a lonely experience. A general rule is that fluent academic writers have a network of writers with whom they share their ideas, early drafts, and polished manuscripts. Now is a good time to develop your network of writers, who inevitably will end up being close colleagues and friends later on in your career.

My hope is that you proceed through this book with a writing group, either in the form of a formal seminar or an informal gathering of classmates. Toward the end of most chapters, I include a section called Group Exercises. I assure you that working through this book and the group exercises with others is not only more effective, it is also more fun. You can learn from one another, encourage each other through the rough times, and share a few good laughs. If you do not already have a group, may I suggest that you recruit a few friends and form one? Informal writing groups work well with four to six students. Formal seminars seem to work best when they are capped at twelve to fourteen students.

If your department does not offer a dissertation writing seminar, take this book to your adviser or the director of your doctoral program and request that they offer one. The faculty member who facilitates the seminar does not have to be incredibly prolific; she could be, but she could also be in a position where she wants to jump-start her research, perhaps after a time in administration or after shouldering a heavy teaching load. Her writing output is less important. What is more important is that the faculty member is comfortable enough with her writing process to share her personal experiences and struggles with writing. This honesty will facilitate students being honest with her and with each other, which makes the seminar more effective and more fun.

If you have aspirations to pursue an academic career, chances are writing will be an important part of your being competitive in the job market and flourishing as a faculty member. If you are pursuing a doctorate as professional development, you may write reports and other lengthy writing projects in your career. Whatever your future holds, learning habits of writing fluency will help you complete your dissertation in a timely manner and set you up nicely for the next stage of your career.

1.3. Data on Ph.D. Completion Rates

If you have been accepted into a doctoral program, then you can complete the degree. Not all students do, but all can. I agree with many scholars of graduate education who believe that our current system for training doctoral students is incredibly wasteful. We have high attrition rates for some of our most successful and strongly recruited students.

Old estimates were that 50% of all students who enter doctoral programs finish; according to a 2007 preliminary report prepared by the Council of Graduate Schools' Ph.D. Completion Project, 57% of students complete their degrees.[1] The completion rates are highest in the engineering and science fields, followed by the social sciences, and then by the humanities fields.

I will state my biases up front: I would love to see every student who enters a doctoral program leave with his or her doctoral degree. If along the way students decide that continuing with their program is not right for them, I would like them to reach that conclusion as soon as possible, leave with a terminal master's degree, and get on with the rest of their lives.

Because I am pitching this book toward humanities and social science students, I will focus on the persistence rates in those fields. Let us look at the statistics for the humanities fields (see Figure 1.1). At three years into their program, it is not surprising that very few humanities doctoral students have completed (3%), a fair number have opted out (15%), and the vast majority of students are continuing with their degrees (82%). At the ten-year mark, the numbers look considerably different. At this point, just under half of all the students have completed their degrees (49%), a fair number are continuing (19%), and almost one-third (32%) have opted out.[2]

Focusing just on the percentages for those who opted out (see Figure 1.2), 15% opted out by their third year and an additional 6% opted out between the fourth and sixth years, for a total of 21%. Between the seventh and the tenth years, an additional 11% opted out, for a total opt-out rate of 32% after ten years. On average, 11% of doctoral students

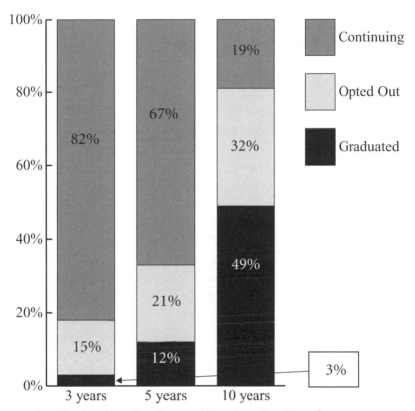

FIGURE 1.1. Graduation, Opt-Out, and Continuation Rates for
Humanities Fields

in the humanities presumably completed their coursework, passed their
comprehensive and qualifying exams, spent a few additional years matric-
ulated, and left without earning their degrees. Well, I don't know about
you, but I think that too many students are opting out. I also think that
far too many are leaving without their doctoral degrees after spending
too much time in graduate school.

In the social sciences (see Figure 1.3), a few graduated within three
years (7%), 16% opted out, and the majority (77%) continued in their
programs. By the tenth year of graduate study, more than half of the
students had graduated (56%), more than a quarter had opted out (27%),
and 17% were continuing. Focusing on the opt-out data (see Figure 1.4),
16% opted out by their third year and 6% more opted out by their sixth

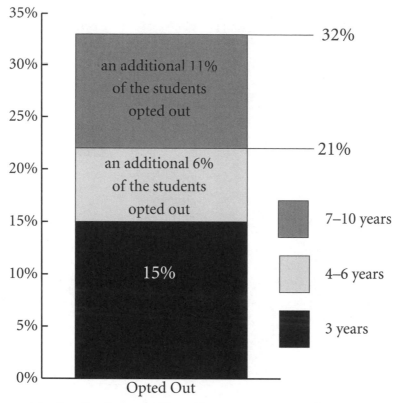

FIGURE 1.2. Opt-Out Rates at 3 Years, From 4 to 6 Years, and From 7 to 10 Years for Humanities Fields

year, for a total of 22%. From their seventh to their tenth year in graduate school, 5% more students opted out. By the tenth year, 27% of all social science students opted out of graduate school. Of this 27%, the majority of the students (16%) opted out within the first three years. After investing six or more years in a doctoral program, 5% of social science students opted out compared with 11% of the humanities students. Although these numbers certainly could be better, they tell us that in the social sciences, the students make decisions about opting out earlier, typically after the coursework is completed but before spending too much time on a doctoral dissertation that they will not complete.

I show you these data to let you know that the high opt-out percentages for highly selected students provide evidence for systemic deterrents

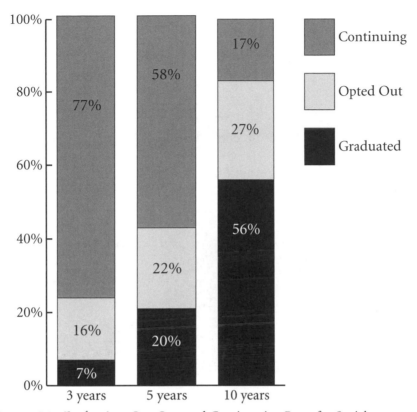

FIGURE 1.3. Graduation, Opt-Out, and Continuation Rates for Social Science Fields

in doctoral training programs. I want you to know about these deterrents so that you are better prepared to overcome them. For instance, onerous comprehensive exams and language requirements, more common in the humanities fields, can drag out the time-to-degree for the doctoral degree and serve as a deterrent to graduating. If you have not already done so, I suggest that you find out as much as possible about the qualifying and comprehensive exams you will be taking. Learn the standards for assessing these exams. Talk with advanced students; ask them to share with you their strategies for success. If you are an advanced student, be generous with passing along to the newer students the tacit rules for successful completion of these requirements.

Not surprisingly, program quality is associated with time-to-degree.

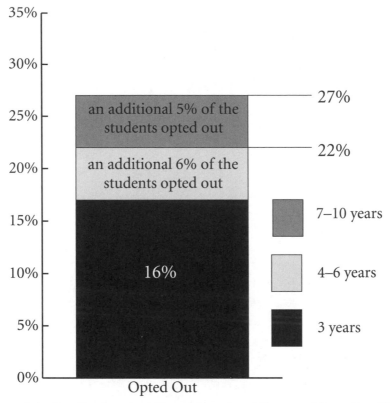

FIGURE 1.4. Opt-Out Rates at 3 Years, From 4 to 6 Years, and From 7 to 10 Years for Social Science Fields

The Center for Innovation and Research in Graduate Education (CIRGE) found that students who graduated sooner were in departments that rated higher on an inventory of program quality.[3] Program quality was measured based on assessments of whether the department provided clear program requirements, preparation for qualifying exams, support and guidance during dissertation writing, financial support, and academic career preparation, among other characteristics. If your department provides this type of support for you—great! If not, then you will need to go out and find it. As suggested earlier, advanced students (especially those who are progressing well) can provide you with some of the information, and perhaps support, you are not getting from your department. Other places to look include the university Center for Teaching and Learning, the graduate college, and professional societies. These organizations may provide professional development programs and support.

Another deterrent is the overreliance on a single adviser as part of the dissertation process. Find out which advisers graduate their students in a timely manner and which ones seem to have a "weeding out" mentality. Having a good working relationship with your adviser is very important; the aforementioned CIRGE report found that students who were "very satisfied" with their dissertation adviser had a lower median time-to-degree than did students who were "somewhat satisfied" to "very unsatisfied."[4]

Of course, you are in control of developing only one-half of this relationship. So keep in mind that, if you switch advisers, switching earlier is better than switching later. Based on your departmental policies, you may not be able to switch advisers. In smaller departments, specializations may be represented by only one faculty member and you would have to switch specializations to switch advisers. Find out your adviser's record for graduating students. If you learn that your adviser's students often take a long time to graduate, you may want to find an informal dissertation adviser to help you move along more quickly.

If you are able to pursue a doctoral degree full-time, the less time you spend in a degree program, the less time you spend living on a graduate stipend. In their first few years, humanities students often support themselves by teaching introductory courses to undergraduates, frequently for partial stipends. Research assistanceships are more available for social science students. If social science students do have a teaching assistanceship, they are often not teaching their own section of a course; therefore they have more time for research.

After a number of years, many students find themselves in a position where they have to increase their income if they are to continue in their degree program. Find out about the opportunities to apply for fellowships and the likelihood that your dissertation adviser would have money to support you. Unfortunately, there exists a dearth of fellowships in the humanities and advisers rarely have grants large enough to support a graduate student.

After a few years of subsisting on a stipend, students may increase their income by teaching additional courses, even up to a full-time equivalent, but without the benefits of being a full-time employee. The very tasks that increase their income can reduce their sustained concentration on degree requirements, such as qualifying exams, comprehensive exams, and doctoral dissertations. The result of this augmented employment is lengthened time-to-degree and the increased likelihood of students remaining ABD.[5] As you move along in your degree program, balance the pros and cons of increased employment. For some, it may be better to tighten their belts while studying for exams and writing their dissertations so that they can graduate sooner. For others, the need for increased employment may cut back on the time they have to focus on their degrees. Make the decision that is best for you.

If you are pursuing your degree while holding down a full-time job, you will quickly find that any extra time you may have had in the past will be long gone. Hopefully, you have a supportive employer who allows you to be flexible in your hours. You may want to schedule time off around your comprehensive and qualifying exams and writing your dissertation. Working full-time while pursuing a doctoral degree can be grueling, and the sooner you can graduate, the better.

If you are pursuing a tenure-track position, time-to-degree becomes a metric that may influence your marketability. Students whose first job after graduation was a tenure-track position had significantly shorter time-to-degree than those whose first job was not on the tenure track.[6] One explanation is that students who had a career goal of obtaining a tenure-track position graduated sooner than those who did not share this goal. Another is that hiring committees rely on time-to-degree as a predictor of scholarly productivity. Probably the best explanation is a combination of the two.

You may have little control over the degree requirements in your department or the opportunities for fellowships in your field; you do have control over your work and writing habits. The sooner you learn techniques for fluent writing, the sooner you will be able to complete your degree requirements. You can apply the habits for fluent writing that we will discuss in this book to studying for qualifying exams or meeting language requirements. The more sustained time you spend on your dissertation (or degree requirements), the sooner you will complete them.

Counter to the popular notions of close mentoring relationships between advisers and students during the dissertation phase, the Ph.D. Completion Project reports that advisers are most available to students during coursework and least available to them for dissertation preparation and the dissertation defense.[7] The reduced support from advisers during the dissertation stage suggests that you will have to obtain this support and encouragement from others, presumably your peers. As I suggested earlier, I strongly encourage you to recruit a handful of classmates and start a writing group. The group interactions will mitigate the isolation that you might experience after you complete your courses, foster the identification of manageable dissertation topics, and serve as proxies for advisers who may be less available to you during your dissertation stage. Meeting with others and discussing your writing habits also helps you to identify the habits that work for you and those that do not. You will be able to solicit suggestions for being more productive and spending more quality time on your dissertation. You will have more time to write and revise prose.

You will find that your writing group participants encourage you to continue when you want to throw in the towel. They will help you sort through problems with advisers, deterrents to accessing sources, and decisions about employment. When you cannot meet face-to-face, you can stay in contact by soliciting feedback on drafts via e-mail, tackling research issues over the phone, or sending encouraging text messages.

While I was revising this book, a friend who is a historian read through an early draft. In the margin, she wrote, "Stress writing groups more." So I am stressing the importance of writing groups, especially if your department's average time-to-degree is on the longer side. Find or recruit a writing group, or sign up for a seminar, and develop relationships with others who will encourage you when you want to quit and will revel in your accomplishments when you graduate.

1.4. The Single System and Prewriting

As I have told my students many times, "Blocking occurs when writers write before they are ready." The best way to prevent writer's block and develop habits of fluent writing is through adequate prewriting. Prewriting is the time you take to familiarize yourself with the literature, identify a focused dissertation topic, take useful notes, and then plan and organize your writing. Prewriting prepares you to sit down and write your first draft.

Writing experts agree on the importance of prewriting. Bob Boice, in *How Writers Journey to Comfort and Fluency: A Psychological Journey*, encourages prewriting by explaining, "Prewriting distributes the usual suddenness of having to generate our best imagining and wording at once." Robert Nash, in *Liberating Scholarly Writing: The Power of Personal Narrative*, uses the term *framing* to emphasize the importance of the work that comes before writing prose: "Framing a manuscript is every writer's inescapable prerequisite for achieving even minimal direction, focus, organization, and clarity in a book, dissertation, thesis, or essay." Bonni Goldberg, a poet, writer, and creative writing teacher, uses the term *percolation* to describe prewriting: "Percolation is the process writers go through before actually writing."[8]

Prewriting is important. The successful writers mentioned here value the time they invest in thinking through a project and collecting the evidence they need to support their claims before starting to write prose. They know that skipping the necessary prewriting steps can lead writers into that dangerous wasteland of writer's block.

I emphasize prewriting because it works. Just as preparation is one of the best antidotes for presentation anxiety, prewriting is one of the best antidotes for writer's block. I stress prewriting because many of my students—and perhaps you—are impatient and want to jump in and write prose before they—and perhaps you—are ready. The time and effort you invest in prewriting—it is an investment—return multifold in terms of writing fluency. For this reason, the majority of this book focuses on prewriting.

After you complete your prewriting—although you never really complete prewriting; you just spend less time on prewriting and more time on writing and rewriting—much of the hard work is still to come. Starting with chapter 8: Developing a Regular Writing Routine, we'll discuss the various aspects of developing habits of fluent writing, which include scheduling writing times, creating an operational writing space, setting deadlines, warding off internal critics, soliciting feedback, and (you knew this one was coming) developing networks with other writers.

My students and I refer to the set of writing techniques presented in this book as the Single System, short for the Single System for Academic Writing. Yes, this term refers to my last name. Although we get a kick out of the literary double-entendre, I do not mean to imply that this system is the only or the best method for describing the techniques of fluent academic writers. The techniques of fluent writers are fairly universal, no matter how you package or apply them. Neither do I mean to be pretentious. Although one of this book's reviewers thought it was pretentious to refer to the set of writing techniques as the Single System, I do not mean it that way and my students have never viewed it that way, perhaps in large part because I am far from pretentious. We settled on the Single System for a very practical reason: It is short. As such, I use this term throughout the book.

At this point, do you need a break to get, or refresh, your large caffeinated beverage? Please do. We have lots of material to cover quickly so that you can get to the important work of writing your dissertation. Figure 1.5 illustrates the Single System and provides an overview of the writing techniques. The Single System starts with interactive reading and note taking. Because these two segments are so closely related, we'll discuss them both in chapter 3, where I present a series of techniques for becoming familiar with a body of literature. The chapter addresses where to start, how to prioritize your reading, and how to network within the field to learn from those who are most influential to the conversation.

I'll use the metaphor of entering the conversation throughout this book. When you are reading and taking notes on the literature in your field, you are entering the conversation, listening and watching. In essence, you are having a conversation with the author. As you begin developing your own ideas for your dissertation, you will be contributing to the conversation. Entering the conversation is a useful metaphor for academic writing because you rely on knowing and understanding the work of others to make a contribution.

Through our discussion on interactive note taking, I present an effective way to take notes. I have spoken with far too many students who have read mounds of papers or books, only to forget what they had read. Other students have said that they remember a finding that they want to cite, but have no idea where they read it. I am a big fan of prevention. Rather than scrambling to find a particularly pithy quote or important finding later, I want you to learn how to take useful notes now. More important, I want you to learn how to take useful notes efficiently. Your notes not only inform your thinking but also facilitate citing and referencing appropriately. This step is essential to your development as a writer and scholar who honors and acknowledges the efforts of others.

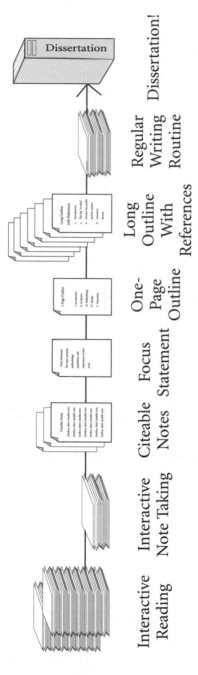

FIGURE 1.5. The Single System for Academic Writing

After reading and taking notes, your task is to distill the work of others so that you can use it to form the foundation of your own work. In chapter 4, I will provide you with techniques for condensing your notes into citeable notes. I named this technique *citeable notes* to emphasize that these notes become the phrases, sentences, and paragraphs that you *cite* in your review of the literature. In general, in social science dissertations you include separate chapters for the literature review, and in the humanities you weave the literature throughout the dissertation.[9]

The next segment is perhaps the most important: developing your focus statement. In chapter 5, called Focusing on Focus Statements, I model developing a focus statement for your dissertation and discuss the importance of being able to state the theme of your dissertation clearly, concisely, and compellingly. The focus statement segment represents the transition you make from entering the conversation to contributing to the conversation. In the interactive reading, interactive note taking, and citeable notes stages, your job is to understand what others have contributed to the literature. In the focus statement segment and the segments that follow, your focus is on contributing to the conversation. The more you share—and inevitably refine—your focus statement, the better. My students have found willing (and sometime captive) audiences in friends, family, pets (dogs are much more attentive than cats), and the lucky person sitting next to them on a cross-country flight.

My dissertation adviser used to say something like, "Have enough good ideas that you can give away a few of them." Not all advisers ascribe to this type of thinking. I have heard of instances where advisers instruct their students not to share their dissertation topics. When I hear of these instances, I am not sure what to say. I regularly tell my students, and I pass this along to you, that whenever the advice you receive from me contradicts the advice you receive from your adviser, the advice of your adviser should always prevail. Based on my working with dissertation writers, however, I find that sharing and receiving feedback on one's topic are consistently beneficial. If you are in a situation where your dissertation adviser tends toward secrecy, try to find out the reason for this secrecy, and then strike a balance between keeping your dissertation adviser happy and getting the support and feedback you need to complete your dissertation in a timely manner.

With your carefully crafted focus statement, you are now ready to plan and organize your dissertation. The one-page outline not only aids in developing a well-organized dissertation, it also serves as a tool to solicit early feedback from your adviser before investing too much time in prose writing. The one-page outline can make your adviser's job and the task of your committee members much easier. In fact, this should be one of your goals. I introduce a theme here that recurs throughout the whole book: Make it as easy as possible for your dissertation committee to think you are doing a great job and to feel comfortable signing off on your work.

Next, we will work on expanding your one-page outline into a long outline with references. The long outline serves as your writing plan, facilitates engaging in a regular writing routine, and assists you in determining when you have read enough in your field.

With your long outline and with references prepared, you are ready to sit down and write your first draft. This is a good place to point out that, although the illustration of the Single System seems to indicate that it is a linear process with a beginning and an end, it is not. You might not begin at the first segment but instead might start midway through the system. Chances are that you will engage in various segments simultaneously. For example, while writing your first draft, you continue to engage in interactive reading and note taking. After writing your first draft, you may go back and reorganize the first half of your dissertation. All along you will be conducting your research or analysis and balancing your time between the research-related and the writing-related tasks.

In the final few chapters of this book I provide guidance on how you can develop a regular writing routine. In these chapters, we will discuss how to schedule and manage your writing time, how to prevent or overcome writer's block, and how to set up an effective writing space. I will present techniques for revising your dissertation so that when you distribute your dissertation to your committee and submit it to your graduate college, you are proud of the work you have done.

If you are going to become a productive scholar, now is the time to develop writing habits that can sustain you through your academic career. Now is the time for you to hone the habits necessary to complete long writing projects with minimal external deadlines and amid multiple demands.

If you are not pursuing an academic career, you can apply the techniques introduced here to other projects. As a professional, chances are you will be writing or overseeing the writing of reports and other long-term projects. You can translate these techniques into careful planning and organizing and into engaging in regular activities that eventuate in the completion of long-term projects. One of my goals is that you learn good habits of writing (and working) that you can take forward as you move beyond the dissertation.

While you experiment with these writing techniques, recruit classmates, start a writing group, and work through this book together. Find friends and colleagues to share your triumphs and your setbacks. Meet weekly or monthly and discuss your reactions to what you are reading in this book. Share your experiences with writing. Be as honest as possible. The members of your writing group may end up becoming some of your closest friends. If you are using this book in a seminar, you are fortunate that your department values the process of writing enough to teach it formally. Appreciate their commitment to you.

On a technical note, rather than struggling through the awkwardness of using gendered pronouns, whenever appropriate I use plural pronouns. When singular pronouns are necessary, I avoid the awkwardness of using he/she, s/he, or him/her. I also avoid using the newly formed but not widely accepted non-gendered singular pronouns, such as ze or hir. To get around this issue, I use feminine singular pronouns throughout the odd-numbered chapters and masculine singular pronouns throughout the even-numbered chapters. When I am creating examples, I refer to the author in the singular rather than referring to a number of co-authors. When using actual examples from the literature, I refer to the author or co-authors, as appropriate.

1.5. Keeping Perspective on Your Dissertation Project

Grades are no longer important, certainly not as important as they were while you were an undergraduate or pursuing a master's degree. Your ability to write a dissertation signifies your ability to enter and contribute to the conversation. Everything you read and write during your coursework, comprehensive exams, and qualifying exams prepares you to write your dissertation. From the very first day of your doctoral program or from the time you read this book, I encourage you to "begin with the end in mind."[10] This phrase is one of the habits that Stephen Covey identifies in his best-selling book: *The 7 Habits of Highly Effective People*. The end, at least for your doctoral program, is a completed and submitted doctoral dissertation.

Nevertheless, I do not want you to over-glorify your dissertation project. I encourage you to view your dissertation not only as the endpoint to your graduate career but also as the beginning of your professional career. Your dissertation should be the worst piece of research that you ever write—not that your dissertation should be bad, but all of your subsequent research and scholarship should be better.

In the spirit of keeping perspective on your graduate career, I offer you a little food for thought. As you read this book, remember and reflect on what a privilege it is to be in graduate school. Whether you are attending a public or a private university, taxpayers are subsidizing your education, as are individual and corporate foundations, alumni, and donors. Even if you pay your own tuition, it is only a fraction of the cost of your doctoral training. It is a privilege to be able to spend time reading the works of some of the greatest thinkers in your field, discussing important concepts, and writing about their work and your ideas. Please do not ever take this opportunity for granted; embrace this time and make the most of it. Enjoy and savor every moment, and then, in your own way, give back to others the privilege that you have received.

As I wrap up this chapter, I want to emphasize that the Single System is not about being perfectly efficient; in fact, it is not about being perfectly anything. This system is about increasing your efficiency, productivity, and enjoyment while completing your dissertation.

Notes

1. John Gravois, "In Humanities, 10 Years May Not Be Enough to Get a Ph.D."

2. Ibid.

3. Joseph Picciano and others, *CIRGE Spotlight on Doctoral Education #3: Does Time-to-Degree Matter?*

4. Ibid.

5. The Ph.D. Completion Project preliminary report and earlier research converge on identifying the factors that influence doctoral degree completion: financial support or lack thereof and relationships with advisers and committee members. See Penelope Jacks and others, "The ABCs of ABDs: A Study of Incomplete Doctorates." and Scott Jaschik, "Why and When Ph.D. Students Finish."

6. Picciano and others, *CIRGE Spotlight on Doctoral Education #3*.

7. Jaschik, "Why and When Ph.D. Students Finish."

8. Robert Boice, *How Writers Journey to Comfort and Fluency*, 74; Robert J. Nash, *Liberating Scholarly Writing*, 67–68; and Bonni Goldberg, *Beyond the Words*, 15.

9. For information about different expectations for the dissertation by fields, see Barbara E. Lovitts, *Making the Implicit Explicit*.

10. Stephen R. Covey, *The 7 Habits of Highly Effective People*.

2

CHOOSING A TOPIC
AND AN ADVISER

In short, you need to become pro-active and take control in order to complete your advanced degree.

—JoAnn Moody, *Vital Info for Women and Under-Represented Graduate Students*

A S EXPERTS LEARN MORE about their fields, they often realize that there is increasingly vast information about their field that they have yet to learn. I am sure, as a graduate student, you have realized that your field is wider and deeper than you realized when you were an undergraduate student. Given the depth and breadth of many fields, how do you go about choosing a dissertation topic? How does that decision influence your choice of advisers? Or is it the other way around? In this chapter, we will discuss the issue of choosing a dissertation topic, an adviser, and committee members.

2.1. A Set of Constraints

The parameters of these decisions remind me of an engineering principle that I learned while conducting research on women in engineering. This common engineering principle states that each problem is solved within a set of constraints. These constraints include resources, time, and knowledge.

As such, I compare choosing your dissertation topic and adviser to planning an engineering project. You choose, if you have a choice, your dissertation topic and your adviser within constraints imposed by your department, university, and field. You will also want to consider how much time you want to invest in the project and what doors it will open for you in the future.

As you contemplate your options, you may also want to do a little soul searching. Why are you getting your doctorate? What are your career goals? What is your professional mission? I would like you to think over your previous academic experiences. What topics piqued your interest? Which specialties caused you to read a little more broadly than was required by your course requirements? Where would you like to make a contribution? What topic supports your post-dissertation professional and personal plans? The answers to these questions often surprise you and most readily reveal themselves while you are talking with others. These answers can guide you as you consider your options, and the constraints, for choosing a dissertation topic and a dissertation adviser.

2.2. Choosing a Dissertation Topic and an Adviser

I remember the statement of purpose that I wrote while applying to my doctoral program. I wanted to work with adolescents who needed additional support, especially at-risk adolescents. For my dissertation, I ended up conducting a study of the first-year experiences of doctoral students, with a focus on identifying the variables associated with success at the individual level and at the departmental level. During my doctoral program, my interests changed. The most significant factor that influenced my research topic was the expertise of my dissertation adviser. As I mentioned earlier, I had met Bob Boice through my need to improve my writing, and I worked with him on the research he conducted on mentoring. Bob's research focused on helping new faculty members adjust to the varied demands of the professoriate; as such, his research focused on the early years. My dissertation replicated his studies on new faculty, but focused on graduate students. Through the process, I learned much in the way of the subject matter, but far more regarding the skills, attitudes, tacit knowledge, and experiences that influence every area of my work life today.

Doctoral students face constraints in choosing their advisers and committee members. I have known departments where students are assigned their advisers upon entry to their programs and they are expected to stay with these advisers through to their dissertation defenses. In other departments, students are assigned advisers and are expected to switch advisers when they begin their dissertations. Practical reasons may limit your choice of advisers because you may find that only one or two faculty members in your department are working in your area of specialization. Some departments assign whole committees upon entry, some dissertation advisers insist on choosing your other committee members, some leave it up to you. While finding the balance between your research interests and advising opportunities, you have to take into account the norms and opportunities of your department and your field.

Regardless of the constraints you face or faced in the assignment of your adviser, you should think about the following questions while considering an adviser and a dissertation topic:

- Does the adviser have expertise and interest in the topic?
- Which theoretical/conceptual approaches does the faculty member use?
- Which discursive, analytic, or research methods does the faculty member use?
- Is the adviser available?
- Does the adviser have a sense of humor (although not a necessary trait, it will make your dissertation process a little more enjoyable)?
- Do the adviser's dissertation advisees graduate in a timely manner?
- Do the adviser's students accept the types of positions you are pursing?
- Will the adviser have funding to support you?

The answers to these questions will guide your decision about choosing an adviser. They can also help guide you to get outside support independent of your adviser. You are pursuing your degree; get the support and assistance you need to succeed.

In some programs, it is more acceptable to choose your own topic of study. If you are pursuing a professional degree (such as an Ed.D. or a Psych.D.) or a research degree in a professional field (such as business) and based on your knowledge built while in the workforce, you may have more latitude in choosing your dissertation topic. The professors in a professional program should appreciate the expertise you have in the field and allow you to build on that expertise to advance your professional training and career prospects. Your constraint, then, is the availability of an adviser who can support your research interests and provide direction on the theories or methodologies that you will apply to your topic of interest.

If you are pursuing a research degree and have the flexibility to choose an adviser, your constraint is also the availability of an adviser. Your program may have only one or two faculty members working in your area of specialization. If your adviser was assigned to you upon acceptance into the program, the expertise of your adviser constrains your choice of topics, theoretical/conceptual approaches to analysis, and research methodologies. The theories and methods you choose will be influenced by those embraced by your adviser and currently in favor in the field.

This is all to say that you must decide, but some decisions will be made for you based on the common practices of your program or field and the availability of advisers. Based on these constraints, I encourage you to balance your own interests with the resources available to you (within the expectations in your department and field) and to work with an adviser who will motivate you through to completion.

I have devised a matrix to help you find the balance between working on a research topic that you care deeply about and working with an adviser. The Choosing a Topic and an Adviser Matrix (see Figure 2.1) takes into account your involvement in the topic; this dimension is represented on the vertical axis. The involvement of a potential adviser is represented on the horizontal axis. While you review this matrix, please keep in mind that it is an oversimplified version of the decision you will face or have already faced. I purposefully chose the vague term *involvement* to represent the range of criteria that you will consider. Involvement can include motivation, knowledge of subject matter, knowledge of theories and methodologies, networking, interest, and current research or scholarship

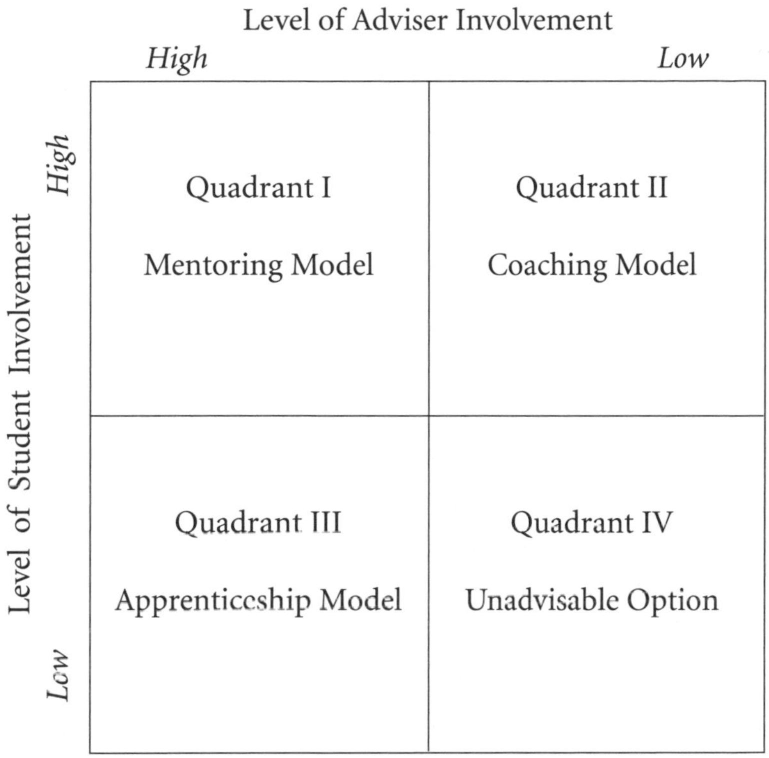

Level of Adviser Involvement

High   *Low*

<table>
<tr>
<td>

Quadrant I

Mentoring Model

</td>
<td>

Quadrant II

Coaching Model

</td>
</tr>
<tr>
<td>

Quadrant III

Apprenticeship Model

</td>
<td>

Quadrant IV

Unadvisable Option

</td>
</tr>
</table>

High

Low

Level of Student Involvement

FIGURE 2.1. Choosing a Topic and an Adviser Matrix

on the topic, among other factors. Because creating a multidimensional matrix would have been tricky in a two-dimensional medium, I developed a two-dimensional matrix and included a host of criteria in the word *involvement*.

As you can see, I identify four options in the matrix, from very desirable to avoid at all costs. The quadrant I option is very desirable. I call this the Mentoring Model. Mentoring occurs when the adviser is very involved in the topic and can inform you on issues related to literature reviews, data or sources, theoretical/conceptual approaches, methodologies, networking with others in the field, and opportunities for presenting and publishing. Your adviser could play an active role in your scholarship or research. Based on your adviser's involvement in the topic, he probably is more invested in your research and scholarship and will presumably be more available to you.

Likewise, your involvement in the topic is very high. For whatever reasons, this topic motivates and interests you. I hope this is at least in part because it overlaps with your professional mission and your career goals. The Mentoring Model represents the best option you could ever conceive of in your doctoral program. If this opportunity presents itself, I advise you to jump on it. If you find yourself in this situation, you should be grateful and consider yourself very fortunate.

Quadrant II and quadrant III are the next best options, but in different circumstances and for different reasons. You should consider quadrant II: The Coaching Model if your interest in a topic is more important to you than is the involvement of your adviser. The adviser could coach you through the practices in your field and assist you in navigating the requirements of your department. Your adviser, however, could not speak to the latest developments in the field, identify areas where the field needs contributions, or introduce you to the network of scholars involved in the conversation.

The Coaching Model is popular or advantageous if you are starting your dissertation work with a considerable amount of research or scholarship experience. You may have entered your doctoral program from a master's program where you learned many of the skills associated with research and scholarship in your field. Or you may find yourself choosing the Coaching Model if developing expertise in a particular topic trumps developing research skills. This may occur if you are pursuing a professional degree and are aligning your dissertation topic with your work experiences, if you are interested in a topic that is understudied, or if you are in an interdisciplinary program. In any of these situations, your level of knowledge and involvement with the subject matter are probably greater than your adviser's. You would rely on your adviser for direction while conducting the research and writing the dissertation.

For example, Antonio Cuyler selected the Coaching Model for his dissertation experience. He earned his Ph.D. in Art Education/Arts Administration from Florida State University. As an undergraduate student at Stetson University, he majored in Voice Performance and Foreign Languages (French, German, and Italian), and for his graduate work he studied Arts Administration. His dissertation examined the career paths of non-European-American executive opera administrators in the United States. His adviser provided invaluable support to help him identify a conceptual model and apply qualitative methods, but she knew little about opera or opera administration. Although Antonio was the "student," he served as a teacher to his committee members, teaching them about opera and opera administration.

He also taught them about the experiences of non-European Americans in arts administration. As a person of color whose adviser was White, he was forging new ground by examining the severe underrepresentation of people of color in opera administration and their experiences. Because the majority of faculty members at doctoral granting institutions are White, this is not an uncommon experience for African or Black Americans, Latinos and Latinas, American Indians, Native Peoples, and Asian Americans who want to study the experiences of people of color as part of their dissertation research.[1]

Similarly, graduate students who pursue a degree in an interdisciplinary field may find themselves relying on their advisers for direction in terms of field-specific knowledge and socialization but forging new ground in terms of accepted methods and standards within their field. Pablo Bose earned his doctorate in Environmental Studies at York University in Canada. His adviser's expertise was in economics (with an interest in philosophy). Along with providing information about economics, Pablo found that his adviser excelled at teaching him how to be collaborative and to schedule and plan his research. His adviser also provided an introduction to the prominent researchers in the field and offered great career advice when he was in the job market.

For his dissertation, Pablo examined how the tension between the environmental protection of wetlands and the expansion of Calcutta's urban borders affected the lives of the communities originally living in those areas. From his topic, you can see how he needed to pull from various fields. As such, it was a good thing that his committee members had backgrounds in economics, urban studies, political science, and anthropology; three of the committee members had appointments in Environmental Studies. Although all of his committee members had high involvement in Pablo's topic in terms of providing advice and being supportive, he ended up being the expert in terms of applying interdisciplinary research to environmental issues. By the way, Pablo is now an assistant professor in a Geography department.

The Coaching Model proved advantageous for Antonio and Pablo.

They both entered graduate school with a clear sense of the topics that they wanted to study. They examined topics that had previously received relatively little attention or that were in an interdisciplinary field. As such, few individual faculty members would have had the subject matter expertise to be highly involved in the research topic, but many could and did provide advice, socialization experiences, and support.

If, however, the development or enhancement of research, analytical and writing skills, and socialization in the field are important to you, I suggest you choose quadrant III: The Apprenticeship Model. In this model, you seek out a dissertation adviser based on his research expertise or reputation as an excellent dissertation adviser. You work on a project related to his program of research. In this instance, you sacrifice your current interests in exchange for developing research skills, scholarly experiences, and a strong network. After you have developed this expertise, you can pursue your topic of interest later in your career. In this sense, you are apprenticing with a researcher and learning all the skills and knowledge you can before you go off on your own.

This option is advantageous if you plan on an academic or a research career. As a postdoc or as a new faculty member, you could continue with this line of research or scholarship while beginning a secondary line of research where you pursue your own interests. What I have found through my own experience and from witnessing the experiences of doctoral students is that when they work closely with faculty members who are supportive, the adviser's involvement is infectious and increases the interest, involvement, and motivation of his advisee. So very often, what started off as an apprenticeship relationship develops into a mentoring relationship, such as occurred in my case.

As I mentioned earlier, I started graduate school with an interest in researching at-risk adolescents and ended up researching first-year graduate students. I worked on my adviser's program of research but applied his research on new faculty members to research on the experiences of graduate students. Because my adviser was highly involved in the field of higher education, I not only learned from him the burning issues of the field, he also introduced me to a network of scholars. I collaborated with him on presentations and papers. I learned the research skills I needed, which gave me the option of continuing research in this specialization or switching to different topics.

Quadrant IV is the Unadvisable Option. This is the quadrant where you have limited interest in the topic and your adviser has little involvement. Stop! Do not even consider this option for a moment. You will spend long days and nights, caffeinated beverage in hand, working on your dissertation. I have found that at some time, most students consider exiting their degree program. Sometimes your interest in your dissertation topic is the only thing that will keep you going; sometimes it is the support of your adviser. If you cannot rely on either of these situations to keep you motivated, even considering the new round of "energy drinks," I know of no caffeinated beverage strong enough to keep you going in Quadrant IV. Choose another quadrant.

Although working on a self-directed research project can be, and should be, engaging and intellectually stimulating, it will also be challenging. As Richard Reis wrote in *Tomorrow's Professor*, "Much of research is just that, re-search. At times, it will be quite mundane and will surely be frustrating."[2] So, in order to prevent yourself from throwing your computer out the window or torching your stack of sources, you should choose a dissertation topic that will keep you engaged and a dissertation adviser who will help you to persist (of course, keeping in mind the constraints imposed by your department and your field).

2.3. Additional Constraints to Consider

When I speak with those who remained ABD after spending a few years working on a dissertation topic, I am struck by a common theme. They were identified as particularly promising students, and as a result, their advisers gave them too much leeway or encouraged them to write a magnum opus for their dissertation. For example, whereas other students chose manageable dissertation projects by conducting a critical analysis of one author's work, the future ABD students began conducting a critical analysis of three different authors' bodies of work. Please do not fall into this trap. Do your homework on prospective dissertation advisers. Believe it or not, some faculty members engage in a bit of grandiosity, some realistically, and some not. Find out your adviser's track record for working with doctoral students. Your goal is a completed dissertation, not a perfect dissertation topic.

The dissertation is being conducted by a student, you. You are called a student because you are still learning the practices of scholarship and research in your field. You can always continue to work on or expand the topic you addressed in your doctoral dissertation as a postdoc or new faculty member. Your dissertation should be the worst research project you ever conduct. If you complete your dissertation, you will have future opportunities to expand your research or scholarship. If you do not complete your dissertation, those opportunities will be unlikely.

This past semester I added required reading to my seminar. I required every student to read the dissertations of two students who were advised by their adviser or prospective adviser. Most of your reading will be of published work in your field, and a dissertation will look very different from almost anything you read in your courses. Oftentimes, students read the best articles and books, written by the most skillful and established scholars. Although those scholars may be terrific authors now, I can assure you that their dissertations pale in contrast to their current work. By reading the dissertations in your department, you will become aware of the format, quality, and length of acceptable dissertations. Not only do I assign my students to read dissertations because I want them to learn about the formats, I also want to boost their confidence. After one of my students completed this assignment, at the next class he shared something along the lines of "I can do that." Bingo. The assignment served its purpose.

In your doctoral program, you are apt to hear metaphors about the powerlessness of doctoral students. Although I have so far kept this book upbeat, unfortunately sexual harassment, workplace bullying, overt and covert discrimination, and plagiarism by advisers and professors are still alive and well. Each of these has derailed the graduate careers of too many doctoral students, regardless of the students' intellect or motivation. If you find yourself in one of these unfortunate situations, I wish I could tell you that your allegations would be justly addressed by the administrators at your university. Unfortunately, I cannot. Universities are loathe to punish professors who engage in these unethical and illegal behaviors. If you are in an abusive relationship with an adviser, do not keep it to yourself. Seek advice from the director of your graduate program, the departments of equity and diversity, human resources or disability rights, the graduate college, the counseling center, or the union (if the graduate students in your university are unionized). These units can provide confidential support or intervention, when necessary. Oftentimes, your concerns will not surprise them because the adviser may have a track record of mistreating students. You are not powerless; the wider you consider your options, the more power you will have. Your options may include switching advisers (if allowable by department policies and procedures) or as a last resort transferring to a different university.

If you find yourself in this situation, you are not alone. Far too many graduate students have been mistreated and have left programs for which they were more than qualified. If this door is unfairly closed, keep your eyes open and your dreams alive because other doors will open. Take advantage of the help that is available to you, keep an open mind about your future career possibilities, and take care of yourself.

Another constraint to consider is the internal review board (IRB) process. You have to apply for IRB approval if you are using human subjects in your study. The rules for requiring IRB approval have become much more stringent in recent years. There was a time when you did not need IRB approval if you were conducting interviews for an oral history or running secondary analysis on previously collected data. Now you do. You cannot apply for IRB approval until you have advanced to candidacy, which means you have passed all of your qualifying exams and defended your dissertation proposal. If the IRB guidelines cover your research project, you cannot start your research until you have obtained IRB approval. (The exception to this rule is if your dissertation project is part of your adviser's program of research and he has obtained blanket IRB approval.)

The IRB process can be finicky. As early as you can, go to the IRB web pages on your university's web site. Read through the criteria and review the forms you need to fill out. Notice when the IRB review committee meets because many meet only monthly, and be prepared to submit your application as soon as you can. Ask advanced graduate students to let you review copies of their IRB applications.

Especially if you are on a strict timeline, you will want to go into your proposal defense with your IRB materials completed. You may need to update them, but that is okay because it takes much less time than if you were starting from scratch. Your adviser must sign your application, so schedule a meeting with him soon after your proposal defense.

2.4. Entering the Conversation: Subject Matter

I use the metaphor of being in the conversation as a way to consider entering, learning about, contemplating, and contributing to a field, which is what you are doing while working on your dissertation. Through the process, you will shift from being a consumer of knowledge to a contributor of knowledge. To be in the conversation, you first have to enter the conversation. Entering the conversation takes patience, humility, recognition of others' expertise, and a healthy dose of self-awareness.

Imagine walking up to an already formed group during a break in classes. Good conversationalists listen to the verbal exchanges, assess the topic, and determine their ability to add to the topic. Sometimes, entering the conversation means listening actively and not saying a word. Sometimes, entering the conversation means taking your knowledge of the conversation, distilling what you have learned from others, and reiterating what has already been said to ensure that you understand the themes and the direction of the conversation. Sometimes, making an effective contribution to the conversation means leaving the active conversation and obtaining additional information and knowledge. Once you have accrued new knowledge and information, you can reenter the conversation and make a unique contribution. Good conversationalists are savvy about determining where and when there is an opening and take that opportunity to contribute.

Entering the conversation, like conducting dissertation research, is a journey. You can start with the end in mind, but the path is revealed only as you embark on the journey. Along the way, the final destination may change. This may be frustrating for people who would much rather read a crystal ball and know the future. Unfortunately, there is no way around this nebulous phase. In entering the conversation, patience and fortitude serve you well, and frustration and hubris are futile.

After I present the metaphor of entering a conversation as a means for learning about and choosing a dissertation topic, often my students ask me questions along the lines of "But what does entering the conversation look like in terms of learning a new field?" "What actions should I take?" "What should I read?" They express their amazement at the vastness of the already extant literature in their field. They do not see how they will be able to make a unique contribution to their field. My job is to provide them with a system for learning the literature and to help them believe that they have what it takes to make a significant and original contribution.

Figure 2.2, titled Entering the Conversation in a New Field, illustrates my system for entering the conversation in a new field. This system starts with reading material that focuses on a broad view of the field and that becomes increasingly specialized. In this figure, I use an example from social psychology, the field in which I received my doctoral degree. When you are entering the conversation in a new field, you may find it useful to obtain an undergraduate textbook such as an introduction to psychology, literature, education, sociology, natural resources, art history, or economics book. Then, read about your specialization in this textbook.

Look through a few different textbooks and you will notice a large overlap in the information, areas of study, and scholars who are referenced. If you are already working in your field, pick up one of these introductory textbooks anyway and read through it; it will provide a quick refresher and overview. If you do not have an introductory textbook handy, you can get a broad overview of the field by searching in Wikipedia. Although some entries may be incorrect or biased, most of the broad definitions tend to be fairly accurate and could adequately serve the purpose of getting a concise overview of a field. The next step is to obtain a more specialized book. These textbooks focus more narrowly on

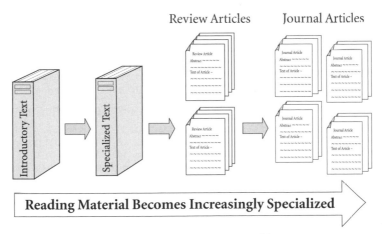

FIGURE 2.2. Entering the Conversation in a New Field

topics such as higher education, twentieth-century art history, or international economics.

I recently pulled out an introduction to psychology text and read through the section on social psychology. The section was 36 pages and discussed the broadest, most widely accepted, and the most influential theories of social psychology. Next, I skimmed through an introduction to social psychology textbook, which included 568 pages of text. This book addressed the topics in a much deeper and detailed manner than the general introductory textbook.[3]

The next step is to identify review materials on your topic. These materials could be review articles or books that provide a contemporary and scholarly examination of your topic. Review papers synthesize the various research or scholarship on a particular topic and present broad themes or overarching findings. I suggest you read the most recently published review papers on your topic of interest. The review paper, or book, can help you efficiently enter the conversation because the literature review should include the latest thinking in the field based on the most widely cited and highly respected literature. Although most review papers focus on the subject matter, some also discuss the accepted theories and methods. If you cannot find a review paper on your topic, look for a review paper focused on a broader topic.

Ask your adviser, your mentor, or advanced graduate students to recommend the journals that publish review articles. If review articles are not common in your field, ask your adviser to recommend specialized readings in your field, which could be published in a book, an edited book, or a compilation of articles or essays.

Continuing with the social psychology example illustrated in Figure 2.2, I would search through *Psychological Bulletin* or *Psychological Review* to find pertinent review articles. These journals include reviews across all the subfields of psychology. If a review paper on a topic in social psychology is published, the journal editors thought the review would be of interest to a broad audience.

Leverage this review paper by looking through its references to identify other articles that address your area of interest. Notice the journals that are widely cited. Then conduct a search for articles that were published in these journals. You will find that your reading material becomes increasingly specialized. The next round of journals would be apt to report on primary research or scholarship. The *American Psychologist* publishes papers on all subfields of psychology, whereas journals such as *The Journal of Personality and Social Psychology* and *The Journal of Social Psychology* publish papers specifically on social psychology.

As an aside, as you read through these materials, I want you to remember that you are reading the highest quality research and scholarship in your field. The author has been writing and conducting research or scholarship for years, if not decades. A lot of caffeinated beverages have fueled his writing expertise. In some fields collaborative work is increasingly popular, so a number of scholars contribute to one article. Although these reading materials are a good way for you to enter the conversation, they are not good standards by which you should assess your own work. Remember that for your courses and for your qualifying or comprehensive exams, you are reading the best in the field.

While you read in your field, make sure you rely on your dissertation adviser as a resource. If you have a list (or stack) of papers and books to read, why not take the list into your next meeting with your adviser? Ask him to help you prioritize which ones to read first and which ones you can skip. Of course, ask him for suggestions, especially for suggestions of his own work if your dissertation topic overlaps with his research and scholarship.

If review papers and journal articles are not common in your field, but books are, then follow the same process while entering the conversation, moving from the general to the specific. Chances are you have read many of the general or overview books as required reading in your courses or from your reading list for exams. Based on the number of books typically included in a reading list for comprehensive and qualifying exams in the humanities, you probably have already read many of the specialized books in your field. Through this process, you entered into the discourse, commentary, and conversation in your specialization.

As your reading becomes increasingly specialized, you enter a more focused conversation. As you identify the scholars contributing to the conversation, do not be afraid to look up their web sites, send them e-mail, and ask them for their current work. Attend conferences and workshops to meet those contributing to the conversation in your field.

Chances are that by the time you are deciding on a dissertation topic, you have already written papers for courses that focus on your topic.

Actually, you may have entered graduate school with a clear idea of the topic you want to study and have been assigned to an adviser whose scholarship incorporates that topic. The earlier you focus on a particular dissertation topic, the sooner you can direct your coursework to writing parts of your dissertation. Then you can use papers that you wrote for courses as chapters or sections in your dissertation.

After reading my plan for entering the conversation, please do not rush out and take my advice in a vacuum. As I regularly tell my writing students, "I am not your gatekeeper; stay close to your gatekeepers." What does that mean? The first person for whom you are writing your dissertation is yourself. The next important audience is the three to five faculty members—gatekeepers—who will approve your dissertation. Make sure you verify that the advice I am presenting in this book works for them. Although the specific techniques may not work, identify alternative techniques that serve the same underlying purposes.

2.5. Examples of Dissertation Topics

Unless your dissertation adviser hands you a dissertation topic, you will choose a topic to work on for a considerable length of time. The decision is quite important. Being in the conversation helps you focus on a topic for which you could stay motivated, at least through the completion of your dissertation. Although I provide some neat and tidy methods for entering the conversation and identifying a dissertation topic, this process can be anything but neat and tidy. Ask every available doctoral student about the process they went through to identify a specific dissertation topic. Following are examples I have compiled of doctoral students' broad interests and their related manageable (and completed) dissertation topics:

- Experiences living on an Indian reservation resulted in a study of the impact that termination and subsequent restoration of federal recognition had on Indian identity as experienced by a particular tribe (Anthropology).
- An interest in the periodical essay, an obscure British literary genre from the eighteenth century, resulted in a dissertation examining its

various forms and how these forms influenced Scottish and American society during the 1700s (English Literature).

- Interest in Black women's role in the civil rights movement resulted in a dissertation illustrating how beauty parlors served as vital locations for transmitting messages and organizing events (African American History).
- An interest in classical literature resulted in a dissertation that examined how philosophers, such as Plato and Aristotle, used rhetoric and argument to "market" their particular brands of philosophy and their philosophical schools (Philosophy and Classical Literature).
- Ponderings on the experiences of Latino migrant workers resulted in a study examining the impact of remissions on the home and host communities of migrant workers (International Economics).

Transforming an interest into a dissertation topic is not an easy task. Be prepared to spend hours reading in your field and specialty area and talking through ideas with classmates and faculty members. You will identify and then discard a great number of possible dissertation topics before you settle on the one that you will pursue. Within the opportunities and constraints that you have, give yourself the necessary time to choose a topic and an adviser wisely.

As you are entering the conversation and considering your dissertation topic and adviser, keep these questions in mind:

- How does this work relate to my professional mission?
- Is there a recent dissertation written on the topic? (If so, this may cause you to shift or change your topic based on the focus of the dissertation.)
- Is there someone in my department with whom I could work on a project within this field?
- Would this topic motivate me for the duration of working on a dissertation?
- Would pursuing this topic serve as a stepping stone to the next phase in my academic or professional career?
- Do I have the resources to complete this dissertation topic within a reasonable time frame?

2.6. Entering the Conversation: Theories and Methods

While entering the conversation, be sure to notice more than just the information being discussed. You also want to notice how information is added to the conversation. One of the most formal and well-known methods for governing a conversation is by using Robert's Rules, which is a set of guidelines that dictate a systematic way for people to participate in a meeting. Another convention we are all familiar with is raising your hand and having the teacher call on you to answer a question. Mind you, you would not raise your hand while sitting down at the Thanksgiving dinner table, so make sure you match the rules for contributing to the situation.

Learning and appropriately applying the theories, conceptual approaches to analysis, and discursive, analytical, or research methods in your field are essential prerequisites of becoming a scholar. Learning the theories and methods is also an essential prerequisite for completing and defending a dissertation. When you read the literature in your field, examine how the data are collected, the sources chosen, the philosophical questions selected, or the texts identified. Take note of the theories and methods and how authors introduce and describe them. Notice how the problems, questions, theories, and methods are matched.

I also want you to sign out a few dissertations from your department's library and examine which theories or methods the authors applied. I suggest that you notice how the writer communicated that he was well versed in the conversation regarding theories and methods. For example, did he include this information as a few paragraphs in the introductory chapter or in a stand-alone methods chapter?

The accepted theories and methods are simply the way that a field has determined that new knowledge can be added to it. That's all. Even if you do not understand the particulars of the theory or method being applied, you should be able to understand why and how it was used. If not, I would argue that the author of whatever you are reading did not do his job. Research is about clearly communicating what you are studying and how you are studying it.

Often, the accepted methodologies are based on historical precedence. In certain fields, it is more difficult to embrace new methodologies than it is to accept either new theories or new knowledge. Often, researchers develop new methodologies in response to new questions or issues raised in the field.[4] And whether we like it or not, different methods have different legitimacy and hierarchies in the various fields.

As a general rule, the most marginalized topics are usually the ones most open to new methodologies. Why this is I can only speculate. I think that these fields had to wrestle with assumptions around power and prestige and came to the conclusion that the currently accepted theories and methods may be restrictive. For example, in anthropology and education, scholars who focused on feminist and minority issues or who supported graduate students interested in these issues were the first to embrace narrativistic scholarship.[5]

Being a maverick in the academy is not without risks. Research conformity is alive and well and rewarded. If you choose to buck the system in your field by using newer or less established approaches or methodologies, go for it. Just be aware that the quality of your work may need to surpass the work of other graduate students. Also, be aware that the intrinsic rewards may be great, but the extrinsic rewards may not be aligned with the importance of your topic or the rigor of your scholarship.

I do not endorse the use of one methodology over another. But before you commit to applying a particular theoretical/conceptual approach or methodology, assuming that you have a choice, I suggest that you talk with a few different professors on its acceptance in your field and how it will influence your marketability. Find out which theories and methods are accepted and mainstream and which are on the cutting edge. Cutting edge can mean up and coming, very prestigious, and accepted. Cutting edge can also mean that the theory or method is gaining acceptance but with skepticism and misgivings. Only after you have acquired this information can you make a well-informed decision.

I am not discouraging the use of cutting-edge or emerging research methodologies or modes of criticism. Rather, I applaud them as contributing new, often egalitarian, techniques for adding knowledge to a stodgy or stuffy field. I just do not want you to get any surprises. Rather, I want you to know that the academy is somewhat value-laden when it comes to evaluating research and writing. I want you to make informed choices for yourself, informed choices that align with your professional mission, scholarly skills, and opportunities within your home department. To inform yourself about the theories and methods in your field, I suggest that, while you are reading, you keep these questions in mind:

- Which theoretical/conceptual approaches of analysis are currently popular? Which discursive, analytical, or research methods are in wide use? What is the reason for their popularity? Which are popular in your department?
- Are certain theories or methods aligned with specific specializations? Certain topics?
- When the same subject matter is examined, how does the choice of theory or method influence the conclusions and interpretations?
- Which approaches/methods are best suited to prepare you for the next stage of your academic or professional career?

In sum, choosing a dissertation adviser is the most important decision you make as a doctoral student; depending on your degrees of freedom around this decision, choose wisely. Determine what your goals are for the dissertation. Do you want to learn the skills of a researcher or do you want to pursue a particular topic? That decision will influence whether you employ the Apprentice Model or Coaching Model. Of course, if you can pursue both, great—choose the Mentoring Model. Make sure your topic is narrow enough that you can complete the dissertation in a reasonable time frame and so that you can become the expert on the topic. Make sure the topic is broad enough that it is appropriate for a dissertation-length monograph and, if you are considering an academic career, can fuel a future program of research or scholarship. Use your dissertation as a stepping stone toward the next stage of your career.

2.7. Managing Your Adviser and Your Dissertation Committee Members

Yes, you read this section heading correctly. In this section, we discuss managing—yes, managing—your adviser and committee members. I originally placed this section toward the end of this book, but several of my students suggested that I move it toward the front, so I took their advice. After you have chosen your adviser, or have had your adviser chosen for you, you have to manage your adviser. You will also have to choose the other members of your dissertation committee and manage them as a group. As you are managing your dissertation adviser and your committee members, I want you to keep in mind that your committee members are very busy people and that it is your job to manage your dissertation process. If your adviser and committee members make managing the process easy for you, consider yourself very fortunate. If not, you need to put in extra time and energy and employ more finesse to defend your dissertation in a timely manner.

After you have chosen your adviser and dissertation topic, how do you choose committee members? In some departments, you do not have a choice. Your committee members are chosen for you by the department administration. Or you may be limited by the faculty members who have specializations in the fields that you need represented on your committee. If you do have flexibility in choosing committee members, I suggest that you discuss this issue with your adviser as soon as possible. Some advisers like to hand-pick their students' committee members; I happen to fall in this category. I know that professors are human and I choose colleagues to serve on my students' committees who hold the students to a high standard while providing them with the support to meet that standard. I also choose colleagues who treat my students with the utmost respect, which includes reading drafts and providing feedback in a timely manner. When I agree to supervise students, I tell them that this is one of the criteria of working with me. If they choose not to work with me, that is fine, no hard feelings; they can find a supervisor who is better suited for them.

Other advisers have you select your own committee. Of course, ask your adviser for suggestions. Then solicit advice from advanced doctoral students and recent graduates from your program. The advanced students and alumni have the surest knowledge of how faculty members treat students. They can let you know which potential committee members respond to students in a timely manner and which ones drop off the end of the earth every now and then. Ask about any personal or professional rivalries that exist among faculty members so you can avoid having two arch enemies on your dissertation committee.

I recommend that you attend a few dissertation defenses before you choose your committee members. Actually, I recommend that from your first year of graduate school you attend these. As you attend, you will start to see which faculty members end up on dissertation committees more often and which ones do not. As a general rule, stay away from the faculty members who are not actively on dissertation committees. Also notice how the outside chairperson (if you need an outside chairperson) runs the meeting. I know of a chairperson who has an incredibly gracious way of running dissertation defenses. She is in high demand.

After you have chosen your dissertation committee, let's skip forward to your dissertation proposal defense. Arrive at your proposal defense with a one-page outline and hand out copies to your committee members. They may have read your proposal a week earlier; they may have read it the night before. The outline provides a shortcut to remind them about your proposal. In chapter 6 we will discuss developing and using one-page outlines.

Keep in mind that meetings such as the proposal defense provide faculty members with an opportunity to discuss ideas, theories, and methodologies. This is what they signed up for. Consequently, whenever faculty members get together, they sometimes get carried away with generating ideas and research projects. They may discuss ways to expand your dissertation project, to add follow-up studies, or to turn your doable dissertation into a ten-year marathon. Remember that they may be enjoying the opportunity to discuss ideas and may not be suggesting that you expand your dissertation project. If this happens in your meeting, and I hope it does, it means that you have an engaged and informed committee.

To avoid agreeing to a dissertation project that will take up the next decade of your life, please practice these two sentences before the meeting: (1) "That is a great idea; perhaps it is something I can do as a follow-up project" and (2) "Interesting idea; is it okay if I discuss it with [fill in name of adviser] to see how it might fit in with my dissertation?" As much as possible, do not agree to a major expansion of your dissertation project during the proposal defense. If the committee members have major problems with your proposal, they (especially your adviser) should have let you know before the meeting. This meeting is meant to get your committee on board and to tweak your dissertation project, not to overhaul it.

Soon after your proposal defense, I suggest that you send an e-mail message to your committee members identifying any changes to your dissertation proposal. Your dissertation proposal is a contract among you and your committee members; you must document any changes to which you all have agreed.

Between your proposal defense and your dissertation defense, make sure to send short monthly or quarterly updates to your committee members. Let them know whether your project is taking a different direction and give them the opportunity to provide input regarding any of these changes. If your expected date of defending your dissertation changes considerably, let them know as soon as possible. Keep these lines of communication open because their situations may change and you will want to know whether they are moving to a different institution or taking an early retirement. If they have not heard from you in more than a year, they may start to wonder whether you are still working on your dissertation or whether you have left the program. The less uncertainty and the more transparency you can provide to your committee members, the better.

In addition, I suggest that you ask your adviser how he would like you to interact with your committee members. Some advisers want you to send out chapters to your committee members when the chapters are not quite polished. Other advisers choose to be the gatekeeper and have you send out only polished or finalized versions of your whole dissertation. After you obtain this answer from your adviser, let the rest of your committee members know what to expect.

If you have set deadlines for distributing chapters or your dissertation to your committee members, as much as possible, meet those deadlines. If you cannot meet a deadline, send an e-mail message to your committee members and acknowledge that you will have the materials to them later than scheduled. Most committee members understand if you a miss a deadline or two. They were graduate students at one point. Nevertheless, colleagues and faculty members who I have talked with across the country regularly share that they do not like when students repeatedly set and then miss deadlines. They translate these behaviors as "not having what it takes" to complete the dissertation. They may get the impression that these students do not value their time or expertise. If you do miss a deadline, be judicious about setting a follow-up deadline and minimize the times that you miss deadlines.

The bigger problem with missing deadlines is not that your professors may believe that you do not have what it takes, but that you may start to believe that you do not have what it takes. If you have a history of missing deadlines, do not worry. As you improve your writing habits; work on the techniques of prewriting, writing, and rewriting in this book; and give and get support from your writing group, you increase the likelihood that you will meet your deadlines. If you are skeptical of whether you can change your writing habits, well, I was too. I did change, and so can you. It takes time and commitment, but you can do it.

As soon as you have a reasonable estimate, coordinate with your committee members to schedule a dissertation defense date and time. Scheduling is a bigger challenge than you may expect. Your graduate college has a deadline by which you must defend your dissertation if you are going to graduate that semester. Keep the date in mind and do not schedule your defense for that week. If your committee members are on other dissertation committees, that week may be a very busy week for them. Rather, defend your dissertation at least a week prior to this deadline to avoid the rush. I recommend that you avoid trying to defend your dissertation in the summer. Faculty members may be out of town for considerable lengths of time, and often faculty members' employment contracts do not include the summer months.

As soon as you have a dissertation defense date and time, reserve your room. Your department's administrative assistant may reserve rooms for dissertation defenses. If this is not a part of his job responsibilities, he can tell you how to reserve a room. Real estate is in high demand in many universities, so the sooner you reserve your room, the more flexibility you have in choosing a room that suits your needs.

In all likelihood, your graduate college will have explicit guidelines specifying when you must distribute your dissertation prior to the dissertation defense. But knowing the graduate college guideline is not enough. Also find out the implicit expectations in terms of lag time for distributing your dissertation. For example, my graduate college guidelines dictate that dissertations need to be distributed two weeks prior to the dissertation, but the unwritten rule is that you distribute it a month prior to the defense. Your adviser, your committee members, advanced graduate students, and recent graduates should know the unwritten rules—learn these rules as soon as possible.

Most universities require a dissertation defense as part of the requirements for earning a doctoral degree. A few do not; rather, they require that the dissertation be signed off by the committee members and that a real-time meeting is not necessary. If a real-time meeting is required, often faculty members can participate via electronic communications.

Nonetheless, as you assemble a dissertation committee, you need to be aware of your time frame and ask about the future plans of your faculty members. If a sabbatical or a retirement may interfere with them attending the dissertation defense, you may want to consider someone else.

Make it as easy as possible for your committee members to think you are doing a great job. Valuing their time, meeting deadlines, and keeping them updated will increase their appraisal of you and your dissertation.

2.8. Group Exercises for Choosing a Topic and an Adviser

On the first day of my dissertation seminar, I have the students share their dissertation topics or possible topics. From the very beginning, I want the students to develop a network among themselves. In my class, I love when students recommend articles, books, and authors to one another. Often they come in the next week with a stack of articles for a classmate. This is what research should be all about: discussing ideas and sharing resources.

On the first day of class, we also set goals for ourselves. My seminar is elective and students take it at different times in their graduate careers, so I ask the students to identify goals that they would like to achieve by the end of the semester. For some of my students, their goal is to complete their dissertations by the end of the semester. Some decide they want their dissertation proposals completed. Others shoot for the identification of a topic and the completion of a long outline. If you are in a formal seminar, the instructor may set the course goal for you. If you have coordinated an informal writing group, choose and share your own goals.

With my group of highly motivated overachievers, I have to be careful about the purpose for setting goals. The purpose is not to show them that they cannot make their goals; the purpose is to show them that their goals are often ambitious and unrealistic. During the first day, I also tell them that we will be revising our goals midsemester. By setting soft goals and revising as needed, dissertation writers can get a realistic sense of their productivity. For you to develop or improve habits of fluent writing, you will need to increase your self-awareness regarding your writing habits.

Another technique for increasing self-awareness around writing and work habits is to graph the time you spend working on your dissertation. Figure 2.3 shows an abbreviated version of a writing graph that you can use as an example. Don't go crazy creating a perfect graph, just create one that is useful, functional, and keeps you honest. You can record the time when you began your writing in the comments row. By recording the times that you start writing, I hope that you will think about your most productive prewriting and writing times. My best time is in the mornings,

Month: _____ Project(s): _____					1st Writing Goal: _____ 2nd Writing Goal: _____							
Comments, time started, time ended, etc.												
5 hours												
40												
20												
4 hours												
40												
20												
3 hours												
40												
20												
2 hours												
40												
20												
1 hour												
40												
20												
Prewriting & Writing Days:	1	2	3	4	5	6	7	8	9	10	11	12 ...

FIGURE 2.3. Abbreviated Writing Graph

as is true for many writers. However, be sure not to become too rigid with your writing times. I had convinced myself that if I did not write in the morning, the day was lost. With the help of my writing partners, I learned that I could also be productive in the afternoon and evenings— perhaps not as productive as when I write in the mornings, but productive nonetheless.

Along with recording the time, I suggest that you keep track of what you were working on that day. The dissertation is a long-term project and may have few external deadlines. As a result of this long reinforcement schedule, I have found that too many students question their progress and then their ability to complete a dissertation. By graphing, you can record how you have spent time on your dissertation. By recording your accomplishments, you create a record of what you have achieved, even if the final product of the dissertation is still far off. Graphing helps reassure my students and will help to reassure you when the internal critics are raising doubts and diminishing your self-confidence. When you graph your dissertation work, you can prove to yourself, your internal critic, and your writing group that you are putting in time and making progress.

If you cannot or do not write on a particular writing day, I suggest that you write down the reason. I do this for myself. Recently my mother visited for the week and I took a writing vacation. When I look back over my writing graph, I see written across that week "Mom visited!" By writing down the reason for writing vacations, I silence my internal critic before the taunts about falling into old patterns of procrastination begin and before the doubts about my ability to finish the project are raised.

At the bottom of the graph is a row for writing days. I want you to realize that every day is not a writing day, even when you are working on a dissertation. Time off from writing is important. This may be your vacation, a weekend, or a conference. Keeping your dissertation work in perspective is important: Overwork can lead to hypomania and burnout; insufficient work leads to nowhere.

Notice that the time slots are in twenty-minute increments. Believe it or not, you can work on your dissertation for only twenty minutes and still be productive. Of course, many of your writing sessions will be longer than that, but at times you might have only twenty minutes. Working on your dissertation for twenty minutes is better than not working on it at all. By regularly checking in on your dissertation, you can keep it fresh in your mind so that you can think about it while you are doing other things, such as working out, walking your dog, or staring out the window during a boring seminar. Do not underestimate the importance of thinking about your dissertation topic while engaging in other activities. During these times, you will make unexpected new connections among your material or think of your dissertation topic in a fresh way.[6] Regularly thinking through your dissertation topic minimizes your start-up time and makes the next day's writing time more productive.

When I ask my students to record the time that they spend on their dissertation projects, my students always ask me what they should record. "Should I include reading along with writing?" "What about time web searching; should I count that?" "What about meetings with my adviser; do you put that on a graph?" I respond that, early on, I want them to record every minute, every second they spend on their dissertations. By recording every activity, they have evidence of the amount of time they have spent on their dissertation and of how long prewriting, writing, and rewriting take.

Next, I often get questions from my students about how to use the graph; I don't have a specific answer. My students' graphs range from elaborate, multicolored, computer-generated graphs to scribbled single-color graphs. Some graphs differentiate among the time spent conducting research, reviewing sources, attending meetings, prewriting, and writing. Others group all the activities together. The only right way to use your graph is the way that works for you. You, like many of my students, will inevitably change how you use your graph. Give yourself permission to use this tool as it best suits your work style. I will tell you what I tell my students: "Whatever works for you, works for me."

Starting in the second class meeting, we all share our writing graphs with each other. At the beginning of the semester, some students are sheepish about sharing their graphs, especially when it was not such a productive week. When students share their graphs with me and with others, I ask them to verbally annotate what was going on. "Why did you write for six hours on one day and not write the rest of the week?" "Why were you able to spend an hour on your dissertation on Monday, Wednesday, and Friday but not on Tuesday and Thursday?" Their answers provide insights into their writing process, their schedules, and the limitations within which they are completing their dissertations. Their answers provide increased self-awareness about their writing habits and writing process.

On those days when they know they will not be able to work on their dissertations, I ask them to review at least something to keep their brains engaged with their project. Often this means reviewing an outline, reading through the first page of a chapter, or reviewing notes they took on reading materials. I remind them that they can stay productive even in twenty-minute increments.

At the beginning of the semester, I regularly notice that many of the students ascribe to the myth that writing can only be done in large blocks of free time. But many students do not have large blocks of free time because they are teaching courses, fulfilling RA responsibilities, picking up children from schools, or having a weekly dinner with their roommates. I encourage them to stop waiting around for large blocks and to start using the small blocks of time that occur throughout their days.

Often the prewriting and research aspects of dissertation projects do not bring about avoidance and anxiety, but the writing aspects do. So when my students enter the writing and revising stages, I ask them to differentiate this time on their graphs. Over the course of the semester, I encourage my students to smooth out their graphs regarding their writing. As the semester progresses, they are spending smaller but more frequent amounts of time on their writing. In Figure 2.4, I have provided a representation of a typical graph as a student improves his writing habits. By smoothing out their graphs, they are combating the myth that constructive writing (or prewriting or rewriting) can be done only when they have a large block of time. They discuss how working regularly at writing results in more hours, and more productive hours, spent on their dissertations over the course of a week.

The goal is to develop a regular writing routine that keeps you going over the long haul. After all, you complete your dissertation over the long haul. Smoothing out your graph means that you give up the euphoria of writing straight for ten hours or for large blocks of time over a few days. Although you can make great progress in these caffeine-fueled writing sessions, it is equally true that they come with a downside. Because these sessions are stimulated by upcoming deadlines, too often writers leave themselves little time for revision. Too often these euphoric times result

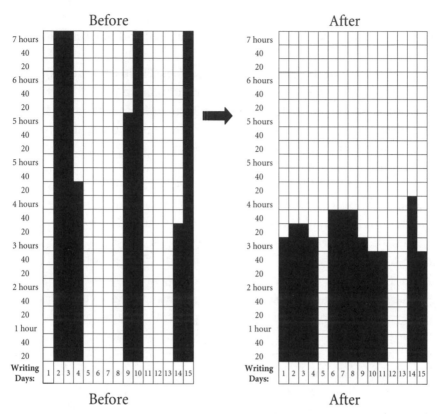

FIGURE 2.4. Smoothing Graphs to Develop a Regular Writing Routine

in an end product that is not up to the standards that you can achieve. Along with a substandard writing product, these "writing binges" can result in health problems, from being particularly susceptible to the common cold to exacerbating chronic diseases one may already be treating.[7] Binge writing also results in an aversion to writing that results in avoidance, until avoidance is no longer possible and you have to engage in another writing binge to meet the next deadline. So use the graph to increase your knowledge of your writing habits and replace the unhelpful ones with helpful ones. Now is the time to develop writing habits that will sustain you through completion of your dissertation and through your future career.

My students hold me accountable to sharing my graph as much as I hold them accountable. I can tell you that my graph is neither color-coded nor fancy. My comments sections are filled with the times I started writing. I record meetings associated with my grants, meetings I often have no control over scheduling. I also record other important activities, such as baking a cake for Valentine's Day, to remind myself why I had a short writing session on a specific day. Thank goodness I rarely have to note that I spent the morning cleaning the kitchen floor; mostly those days are over.

By sharing my graph, I continue to improve my writing habits. In addition, my students quickly learn that I am all too human. I am very honest with my students about my writing struggles, scheduling issues, and the current tenor of my internal critic. On numerous occasions, my students have shared that they appreciate my openness about my writing difficulties. When they are comfortable, they too share their writing challenges with the class.

As you share your graphs with your writing colleagues, you will soon realize that you are the only one who remembers that one week toward the end of February when your graph was completely blank. You will soon realize that the reason to share your graph is not so that others can hold you accountable; it is so that you can hold yourself accountable. You'll realize that when you put the time in, you make progress.

Notes

1. National Center for Education Statistics, "Table 229. Employees in Degree-Granting Institutions."

2. Richard M. Reis, *Tomorrow's Professor: Preparing for Academic Careers in Science and Engineering*, 113–14.

3. Thanks to Susan Varni for lending me her copies of Neil R. Carlson and others, *Psychology: The Science of Behavior*, and Stephen L. Franzoi, *Social Psychology*.

4. See Kuhn's notion of the disciplinary matrix and how paradigm shifts occur when new topics, questions, or issues arise that cannot be satisfactorily addressed by the previous disciplinary matrix: Thomas S. Kuhn, *The Structure of Scientific Revolution*.

5. For example, see Ruth Behar, *Translated Woman: Crossing the Border with Esperanza's Story*, and Robert J. Nash, *Liberating Scholarly Writing: The Power of Personal Narrative*.

6. The field of insight research has provided neurological evidence to support the notion that we often have to stop focusing on a problem to solve the problem. For recent developments in the field of insight research, see Bruce Bower, "Road to Eureka!"

7. Robert Boice, *How Writers Journey to Comfort and Fluency: A Psychological Adventure.*

3

INTERACTIVE READING
AND NOTE TAKING

To get meaning out of a set of words, a reader must build meaning in.

—Peter Elbow, *Writing with Power*

AVE YOU EVER SHUFFLED through a stack of articles, a mound of books, or a pile of Internet printouts, looking for a research finding, a literary text, historical material, or a particularly poignant quote? Have you read a book or article a week ago and then thought to yourself, "What have I read?" Has your reading merged into a great collage of ideas, names, and theories in your memory? If so, you are not alone. The antidote to this situation is active reading and efficient note taking, what I refer to as interactive reading and interactive note taking. These two prewriting techniques facilitate your remembering what you have read and equip you to reference your reading while writing your dissertation.

Although interactive reading and interactive note taking are two segments of the Single System, they are so closely interlinked that I describe them in one chapter. In the illustration of the Single System for Academic Writing (review Figure 1.5), you can see that interactive reading is the first step in the Single System. Interactive reading is symbolized by a stack of papers that represents the thousands of pages you will read while in graduate school. The interactive note taking segment is a much smaller stack of paper and represents the notes you take on your reading.

The acts of interactive reading and interactive note taking facilitate interacting with ideas. The more you actively relate to ideas, the more you remember them. When I write down my parking space, I am more likely to remember it even if I never look at that note again. Likewise, by interacting with ideas in a manner that addresses your assessment of the writing and how you can imagine the ideas influencing your dissertation project, you will remember the ideas much more readily. Because you can access these ideas at any time, you can shuffle them around in your memory while walking to and from your car, walking your dog, or taking a shower.

3.1.   Scholarly Reading Is the Foundation of Your Dissertation

In class when I discuss interactive reading and note taking with my students, I tell them that if they do not take notes on an article or book, do not bother reading it. Many of them look at me in dismay. I continue, "Read a good novel instead." The goal of reading in academe is not only to learn from it, but to be able to use the reading as building blocks in your own work. If an academic article is not important enough for me to take notes on, then I do not read it. I would rather reread one of my Harry Potter books.

Scholarly reading serves a purpose. The goals of scholarly reading are to provide you with an understanding of the conversation, the tools to provide evidence that you are in the conversation, and a foundation from which you can contribute to the conversation. As such, scholarly reading is inextricably linked to effective and, hopefully, efficient note taking. With interactive reading, you can listen to and interact with the conversation in your field. Interactive note taking provides you with a risk-free forum for experimenting with academic writing. As you take notes on others' work, you are writing about your topic and experimenting with your academic voice before your internal critic awakens, before your self-doubts kick in, and before the perdition of writer's block can stop you.

By taking interactive notes, you create a forum for thinking critically about the material you are reading. As you read carefully in your field, you may find that you question the author's conclusions based on her sources or data. Take notes that help you understand the author's point, and take this opportunity to trust your interpretation of the reading. While reading and thinking critically, please do not fall into the trap of being a critic. Published research is hard work and it must undergo rigorous review by peers in the field to be published in a journal or by an academic press. If authors waited to publish until their writing reaches perfection, very few pieces would be published. By and large, and with few exceptions, every piece of published literature has something to offer to you.

Whereas I have been talking about entering the conversation in a metaphorical sense, you can enter—or at least listen in on—the conversation in a tangible sense. For example, a student in my dissertation writing seminar was reading articles in the *Journal of Rural Education (JRE)* because her dissertation research focused on the needs of small rural elementary schools. In an earlier meeting, I had suggested to the students that they contact an author if they are reading anything that particularly piques their interest. Chris took me up on this suggestion and sent an e-mail message to a professor whose articles regularly appeared in *JRE*. He responded and sent her recent articles he had published and provided the names of a few other researchers whom she could contact. When Chris shared this experience in class, we could see how the author's response motivated and inspired her. In an electronic sense, she was in the conversation.

Although I would love to tell you that you will get the same positive response that Chris did, I cannot. Professors are busy people and some can respond promptly to such requests and some cannot. If you find that an inquiry you sent has dematerialized into the ether, just try another researcher. Eventually, you will find someone who has the time and inspiration to respond to your requests.

Engaging in interactive note taking provides you with the building blocks for your own work and facilitates discussions with your adviser and classmates. By taking useful notes, you can refer to the sources, theories, methods, analyses, results, and conclusions of your reading. When you meet with your dissertation adviser, you can bring two copies of your notes and use them as starting points for discussing your dissertation. Sharing your interactive notes with your dissertation adviser can provide an efficient means for her to give and for you to get feedback on your reading. Of course, not all advisers are available for these types of interactions. So make the best of your situation and, if necessary, find like-minded classmates with whom you can discuss your reading.

3.2. Reading Is a Privilege

Another benefit of engaging in interactive reading and note taking is that you will rekindle the joy of reading. Chances are that you once enjoyed reading. Unfortunately, I have met far too many graduate students for whom this earlier joy has become a chore. The time pressures of reading piles of assigned reading have crowded out any pleasure they used to experience. Too often, the amount of reading in graduate school is unrealistic. Taking notes just adds extra time that you do not have.

If you can relate to this situation, then I would like you to think differently about reading. Reading is a privilege. Reading allows you to have a conversation with the author at your convenience. Reading allows you to examine the thinking of some of the greatest minds in your field. What I hope is that, by employing interactive reading and note taking, you will rekindle your love of reading.

I also hope that you recognize the value of prewriting. Scholarship requires that you spend hours reading and taking notes. Now is as good a time as any for you to learn new and efficient techniques that enable you to read and reference mounds of papers and stacks of books. Experimenting with new formats for note taking requires an additional time investment. As you become increasingly facile with these techniques, you will actually spend less time reading and note taking than you did before. Learning these techniques enhances your prewriting productivity and increases your satisfaction with your reading.

3.3. Collect Notes, Not Articles or Books

While engaging in prewriting, do not collect articles or books; instead collect interactive notes. While I was a graduate student, before the ubiquity of the Internet, I had to go to the library to copy articles. One afternoon, after I had been standing in front of a copy machine for a few hours, I had an epiphany. Yes, I know *epiphany* is a strong term, but at the time my brain was so overloaded with reading, ideas, and things to do that any type of productive self-reflection was an accomplishment. I was copying the articles while mentally lamenting that I would only go back to my office and add them to the stack of unread articles on my desk. As I thought about this, I realized that I spent more time standing in front of the copy machine than I spent engaged in interactive reading. I stopped copying articles and began reading them in the library. By doing so, I gained back all that wasted copying time.

As a result of this change, I managed to read many more articles. I also saved a lot of money, at a time when every dime was precious. The pile of unread articles on my desk slowly dwindled. I felt good about myself and my progress every time I walked back from the library. The danger was that sometimes I would have to refer back to an article that was not housed in my file cabinet. But I decided that what I gained by spending my time engaged in interactive reading and note taking more than offset the few times I had to walk across campus to the library to retrieve an article for the second time.

These days, with the Internet, you can access articles and books on your computer, which exacerbates the problem of having more reading material than time to read. As you download articles, read, and take notes, keep in mind that you should continually examine your work habits. Are they working for you? If your work habits are not working for you, change them so that you convert inefficiently invested time into useful time. A large pile of unread articles or books buys you nothing; fewer articles or books carefully read are more useful than a large unread stack.

When you engage in interactive reading, I suggest that you keep a few goals in mind. First, you are reading to provide information that informs your dissertation research. Your goal is a completed dissertation. To write a successful dissertation, you need to learn the expectations, structures, formats, and styles associated with the academic writing in your field. Everything you read informs your knowledge of the expectations and format used in your field. Becoming familiar with the elements of academic writing and the acceptable structure for setting up these elements helps you enter, and then contribute to, the conversation. By focusing on the patterns instead of each aspect or finding as a separate unit, you will shorten the time needed to read and to become an expert in your field. Okay, I know that sentence is vague. Let me provide examples.

Based on research on expert performance, recognizing patterns and leveraging this recognition distinguish experts from novices.[1] Expert chess players view a configuration of chess pieces as one unit and consider a series of future moves, not one move at a time. In contrast, novice chess players see each chess piece as a separate unit and each move as a single event. Expert typists type *the*, while novice typists type *t*, *h*, and *e*. In addition, when expert typists type *the*, they are looking forward to the next words to type.

How does this translate into academic reading? As you increase your ability to understand the meaningful patterns and relationships among the various elements of academic writing, you can decode the writing in your field. You increase your facility to engage efficiently in interactive reading and note taking. Although academic writing looks very different across the humanities and social science fields, it follows some pretty straightforward patterns. The basic pattern is that the author sets out a premise, analyzes sources or data, and then presents conclusions that either support or cause her to revise the premise. Based on the supported or revised premise, the author presents conclusions and implications for the field. The same pattern is used whether a researcher is putting a literary text into a new context, conducting empirical research, reviewing historical records, or writing a review paper (for the review paper the author analyzes and synthesizes articles and books as sources and data).

In an article published in the *American Historical Review*, Tyler Anbinder provides a nice example of putting forth a premise, examining sources, and then either supporting or revising the original premise. In this instance, the author revised the premise. By focusing on the experiences of one woman, Ellen Holland, Anbinder examines the experiences of Irish immigrants who had lived on the Lansdowne estate, the poorest and worst hit area in Ireland after the Potato Famine of the 1840s. Holland resettled in the Five Points district of New York, "the most infamously decrepit slum in North America."[2] In his article titled "From Famine to Five Points: Lord Lansdowne's Irish Tenants Encounter North America's Most Notorious Slum," Anbinder presents his original premise:

When I began investigating the history of Five Points, I assumed that the prevailing, gloomy picture of the famine-era immigrants would be borne out on its mean streets. Given that Five Points' residents were the most impoverished in antebellum New York, I expected to find them barely scraping by from payday to payday.[3]

Through his research, he provides a revised premise:

But the bank balances of Ellen Holland and her fellow Lansdowne immigrants force us to reconsider such long-held preconceptions. . . . whatever such future studies may reveal, a few things are certain. First, the degree of financial success achieved by the Lansdowne immigrants despite their decrepit surroundings suggests that the famine immigrants adapted to their surroundings far better and more quickly than we have previously imagined.[4]

He is able to consider and revise the originally held premise because he had access to newly released original sources. These sources were the records from the Emigrant Savings Bank, the bank in which many of the Lansdowne immigrants deposited their life savings. The bank records were particularly useful because they include not only financial accounts but also "test books." The test books include personal biological information that was used to test anyone desiring to withdraw money to ensure that they were the account holder. In Appendix A, I provide excerpts of this article and annotate the various elements that I introduce later in this chapter. In this appendix I also include a narrative that explains the annotations.

Although the pattern of premise, examine data/sources, support or revise premise is pretty uniform across academic fields (exceptions always do exist), how this pattern is implemented can look quite different. In "Improving the Writing, Knowledge, and Motivation of Struggling Young Writers: Effects of Self-Regulated Strategy Development With and Without Peer Support," an article published in an education journal, Karen Harris and her colleagues investigate interventions for improving the writing performance of struggling young students, students who were around seven years old. When the authors present their premises, they state them as research hypotheses (as opposed to statistical hypotheses)[5]:

> One purpose of the current study, therefore, was to examine the effectiveness of an instructional program in improving the performance of young, struggling writers attending urban schools serving a high percentage of children from low-income families. . . . The second purpose of this investigation was to determine whether social support through peer assistance would enhance SRSD-instructed students' performance, especially in terms of maintenance and generalization.[6]

To examine these premises, the authors collected data by conducting an experimental study. They randomly assigned young students to three groups. One group was the control group who were taught using a widely implemented writing instruction method. The second was an experimental group that was taught writing by focusing on the planning and organizing stages, and the third group received the same intervention as the second group except with an additional social support component. Based on the analysis of their data, Harris and colleagues present a revised premise:

> The present results demonstrate that, as early as second grade, the writing performance and knowledge of young struggling writers can be improved substantially by teaching them . . . strategies for planning in conjunction with the knowledge and self-regulatory procedures needed to use these strategies effectively. . . . Finally, our results show that a common procedure in clinical psychology, peers helping each other maintain and generalize gains, can be applied successfully to academic learning with young children.[7]

For this social science article, I also present excerpts, annotate the various elements of academic writing, and provide a narrative to explain the annotations. You can see these in Appendix B.

If you take a positivistic approach to your analysis, then the premise, analysis, revised premise pattern is very familiar to you. This pattern mirrors the identification of hypotheses, collection and analysis of data or sources, and then the acceptance or rejection of the hypotheses. Even if you use a constructivist approach to research, you still follow this same pattern. Your premise influences your recruitment of participants and development of an interview protocol. Or it influences your choice of sources to examine, theory to apply (if there is a decision to be made regarding theories), and focus that you bring to the research. The constructivist approach certainly addresses the analytic methods you use. Whether you use a positivistic or a constructionist approach, this simple pattern guides the vast majority of academic writing.

Taking something seemingly complex and breaking it down into its essential elements can help you quickly grasp the important aspects of an article or book. Although I contend that the premise, examine data/sources, support or revise premise pattern is widely applied across fields, I do not mean to imply that the history or education examples I use are representative of all the humanities or social science fields or even of their own fields.

3.4. Interactive Reading in Practice

Okay, I have discussed interactive reading and entering the conversation in a metaphorical sense, but what does it look like in practice? I present techniques that I learned from my dissertation adviser and that I have revised based on my experiences and the experiences of my students. I hope that you will try these techniques. Then I hope that you will adapt these techniques to suit you and your scholarship.

When you begin interactive reading, I suggest that you have pencil in hand. I was an accountant in a former life, so I prefer mechanical pencils. Use a pencil to underline the important parts of the articles or books and to write notes in the margins. I suggest using a pencil because it has an eraser. I suggest that you use the eraser freely but not excessively. Remember, interactive reading is part of the writing process; the end product is your completed dissertation. Do not aim for perfection during this step, or in any step throughout the journey. Certainly, do not let perfectionism slow you down as you engage in interactive reading. As such, erase, but do not go overboard. Scribbles and cross-outs in the margins are quite acceptable.

In contrast, I suggest that you do not use a highlighter. This advice may surprise you. Indeed, it routinely surprises my students. Using a highlighter promotes sloppy or excessive highlighting and enables you to read in a superficial manner. Rarely have I seen students go back and reread the passages they have liberally highlighted. It is best to read carefully the first time. Usually, after I finish my rant and rave about the advantages of pencils and disadvantages of highlighters, one of my students expounds on the advantages of highlighters. Okay, I usually give in. The truth is that I do not care what they, or you, use. What I do want is for you to mentally interact with the reading and indicate the important parts of the text to facilitate note taking.

Of course, if you are reading a library book or a book that is not yours, I suggest that you refrain from marking up the pages. I do, however, delight in reading library books where others have added their annotations. In those instances, I imagine that I am in a three-way conversation among the author, an anonymous previous reader, and myself. Apparently, I am not alone in enjoying these three-way conversations because a field of research has developed around "marginalia."[8] Writing in the margins was a very popular pastime in the late eighteenth- and early nineteenth-centuries, and recent scholars have examined the two-way conversations between the books and their Victorian-era readers. Although the marginalia scholars and I may enjoy reading the jottings in the margins, many readers do not, so please do not write in library books.

So, with pencil in hand, you are ready to preread, which provides you with the big picture of your reading. If you are reading a book, then read through the table of contents. I also suggest that you read, or at least skim, through the prologue and introduction because they provide an overview of the book and the author's reasons for writing it. For an article, flip through the article and skim the headings, subheadings, and references before you start reading. As you find out later when I discuss outlines, the headings and subheadings serve as the table of contents for the article. Taking the time to do these prereading steps makes the rest of your reading more focused and also provides you with information that helps you to decide whether or not it is worth your time to read the book or article.

I recommend that you read through to the end of the article, book chapter, or book before you take any notes. I have seen too many students take unnecessarily detailed notes otherwise. Although this is okay if you have unlimited time, you are probably short on time. I want you to learn how to get what you need out of your reading as efficiently as possible so that you can get through your reading, create effective notes, and move onto your research and writing. Completing reading before taking notes helps.

Interactive reading occurs when you have an active conversation with the author. While reading, ask yourself questions about the reading so that you engage actively. Not all of the following questions apply to every field, but as you are reading, ask yourself these types of questions:

- What is the main point or result? Is the point well supported or not? Do the data or the analysis support the author's conclusions and implications?
- Which text, artwork, original sources, or data did the author analyze? How did the author obtain or collect these primary or secondary sources?
- Which theoretical/conceptual approaches to analysis did the author apply?
- Which research methodologies, discursive methods, or methods of synthesis did the author use? Would I consider using these methods for my dissertation?
- How does this reading relate to my academic interests, professional mission, current projects, or future plans?

Keep these questions in mind as you jot down thoughts in the margins, underline passages, and put codes next to important sentences. When you are writing your interactive notes, rely on your underlining and margin notes to jog your memory regarding the important aspects of your reading.

When I read an article, and most of the time I read articles from the social sciences, I usually put three asterisks next to the main point. When the author gets specific about her hypotheses, I put H#1 or H#2 next to those sentences. I note the theory by writing "Th" next to the section where the author discusses it. If I see a quotation that I particularly like, I underline the whole quote and put a "q" next to it. If I have any questions, or critiques, I write down questions marks. The number of question marks reveals the intensity of my bafflement or disagreement. These margin notes can range from "?" to "?!?!?!" I read through and annotate the whole article before taking any notes.

While reading a book or any long work that you own, I suggest that you not only underline and use margin markings, but that you also write preliminary notes on a sticky note and post it to the inside cover of the book or document. If you do not own the source, then rely on sticky notes and tabs so that you can quickly turn to the pages from which you will take notes. On the sticky notes, write phrases such as "Hypothesis of book page 23," "theory p. 63," "Good quote p. 103," and "Chapter 3 is important for my work."

In some instances my recommended techniques for engaging in pre-reading and interactive reading may not serve you well. For instance, if your primary sources are on microfiche, it may be inconvenient and inefficient to read through the full source first and to take notes afterward. If you are traveling abroad to review a manuscript, you may choose to trade off efficiency for thoroughness by taking very detailed notes; the opportunity to review the manuscript at a future time may be prohibitive based on travel expenses and access fees. In these instances, consider the underlying principle and modify the reading and note taking techniques to suit your situation. The underlying principle is to develop efficient work habits for yourself that move you closer to a completed dissertation. In short, I want you to start reading with a plan, interact with the reading, and take useful, brief notes.

While you read in your field, remember that the dissertation is a unique animal. Often (too often in my opinion, but this is changing), dissertations are extensively revised before being published as a book or a series of articles. So your job is to learn the conventions for publishing in your field as well as the conventions for writing dissertations. While you engage in interactive reading and note taking, I suggest that you sign out two dissertations from your department. (Have I suggested this already?) Make yourself a large caffeinated beverage, sit on a comfortable seat, and read them. As you are reading, notice the organization and format of the dissertations. Examine how the authors present the main point. How do the authors communicate to you that their work is important and that you should care about it? Which theories or methods do they apply? As you read the dissertations, you will see that they follow certain patterns and formats, patterns and formats that you will use when you write your dissertation.

As you are reading in your field, I also want you to notice how your field reports others' work using *reporting verbs*. In an interesting pamphlet called *Writing in the Academy*, Ken Hyland states, "[E]ngineers *show* while philosophers *think*, biologists *describe* and linguists *suggest*."[9] Based on his research on academic genres, he finds that the most frequently used reporting verbs in philosophy are *say*, *suggest*, *argue*, and *claim*, and sociologists report on their research using the verbs *argue*, *suggest*, *describe*, and *discuss*. Applied linguists most frequently use the reporting verbs *suggest*, *argue*, *show*, and *explain*, whereas marketing experts use *suggest*, *argue*, *demonstrate*, and *propose*. In addition, note how writers report on their findings. As a precautionary note, avoid anthropomorphizing studies or reports. I have read quite a few dissertations where particularly clever *studies showed* or *reports demonstrated*. To prevent this problem, I suggest that you write something like "In this study, the *authors showed* this amazing finding" rather than giving the study all the credit.

As you engage in interactive reading, note the limitations of the scholarship or research that you are reading. By thinking critically about pre-eminent work in your field, you will learn that even the highest quality scholarship is not perfect. If this is a shock, I hope you are sitting down because here comes another one: Your dissertation will not be perfect. You, and all scholars, conduct and publish research and scholarship within the constraints of living in three-dimensional space. Write the best dissertation you are capable of writing now, and move on to publish higher quality research and scholarship in the future. Please do not get caught up in being perfect at this stage of your career because you have a long career ahead of you.

3.5. Using a Bibliographic Program to Record Interactive Notes

When I first taught my dissertation writing seminar, I encouraged my students to limit their interactive notes to just one page, whether the reading was a journal article or a hefty book. Now we use a bibliographic software program to record our interactive notes. Nevertheless, I still encourage my students to be succinct and concise in their note taking. My students and I use the EndNote[10] bibliography management tool because our university has a site license and we can download the program for free.

Of course, you can use other bibliographic programs. Click around your university's web site to see if it offers a site license for one of the many bibliographic programs on the market. If not, order one through your bookstore or download one from the web. Popular bibliographic programs include Reference Manager, ProCite, and Bookends. In addition, you can download free bibliographic programs that are licensed under the GNU General Public License, such as Bibus or RefDB. If you want to, do look over your options. Wikipedia has tables comparing the various programs.[11]

If you do not already use a bibliographic program, get one now. If you are not using one, you are handicapping yourself. Bibliographic programs are valuable because they automate the process of developing Bibliographies and Works Cited or References lists. If you delete a citation at the last minute, the bibliographic program automatically drops it from your bibliography. But that is not all. You can also use your bibliographic program to organize the electronic versions of the literature and to store your notes on this literature.

Once you familiarize yourself with the bibliographic program you are using, the rest of this chapter will make more sense. I am sure that if you are using a bibliographic program different from EndNote, it has the same functionality, just different menus or fields.

When you enter a new reference and interactive note, choose one field for your interactive notes and, as I discuss in the next chapter, one field for your citeable notes. If you are using EndNote, use the fields shown in Figure 3.1 on the EndNote reference page. These fields are Keywords, Abstract, Notes, and Research Notes.

If you ever want to create subsets of your references, you can sort on the Keywords field. For the sort to be useful, be sure you enter keywords judiciously. Too many makes any subgroups meaningless; too few provide inadequate subgroups. I suggest that you reserve the Abstract field for the abstract and any or all parts of the article or manuscript. With more scholarly journals and texts online, you may be able to find electronic versions. If you can copy the abstract and text, you can paste them into this field or add a link to the location where you saved the article on your hard drive. Download the article and save it on your system so that you do not have to depend on having Internet access to read the article. This way, as long as you have your laptop, you have access to your articles and can read them anytime and anyplace. In addition, you can organize

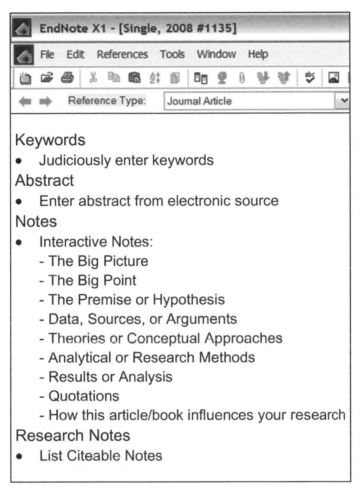

FIGURE 3.1. EndNote Template

pictures or objects in EndNote by using the Audiovisual Material reference format. Of course, make sure you record the information you need to request copyright permission, if necessary.

Many times you might cite only the finding or conclusion of an article or book. There will also be plenty of times when you want to set the findings or conclusions in the context of the research or scholarship. To do so, as part of your interactive notes, record the *big picture*. The big picture is the context for the work, and all academic writing addresses it.

Examples of the big picture are the historical or political landscape, the progression of research on a particular topic or argument, and the development and refinement of a theory. Whatever the author is presenting, she has to provide for the audience the larger setting or situation within which her scholarship resides.

Also record the *big point*. The big point addresses the question: "Why is this research important?" Pay close attention to your field's practices for communicating that research is important. In some fields, it is perfectly acceptable and even preferable to telegraph the big point by writing: "This research is important because . . . " Other disciplines may require more nuanced ways to communicate the big point. Keep this in mind because in the introduction of your dissertation you will communicate to your dissertation committee and wider audience why your dissertation research is important. Do not compel your audience to read your mind and do not dance around this issue. Be as straightforward as you can, within the acceptable directness of your field.

The premise or hypothesis is a version of the big point that focuses squarely on the research being conducted. Next, record the data, sources, or arguments that were researched or addressed in the reading. In short, this is the unit or units of analysis. The analysis could have utilized data, the writings of a particular author, an untranslated manuscript, a longstanding philosophical problem, or the progression of a particular theory.

You may need to record the theories or conceptual approaches the author applied to the analysis. Depending on your field, this may be very important or not at all relevant. Similarly, when you record the analytical or research method, for some fields you need to be very detailed in your description; in others, the prevailing methodologies are widely known and applied and require little description.

All of this information helps to set the stage for the results or analysis, which, of course, you want to include in your interactive notes. I skip over the Quotations field for now and encourage you to include a section on how the reading addresses, informs, and supports the need for your dissertation study. Please do not skip this step and expect that just thinking about it is enough. Rather, this section provides you with a forum for thinking about, and writing about, your dissertation well before you are ready to write formal prose. Plus, you will be surprised how what seemed so obvious while reading a book or article so readily slips out of your brain after reading a zillion more pages. So write down your thoughts now so that you can use them later.

Admittedly, I have only briefly touched on these various elements because they vary widely across fields and because you have spent a considerable amount of your coursework addressing the different elements of academic writing, research, and scholarship in your field. Interactive reading and note taking follow the same format, so you can review Appendixes A and B to see how the elements that you record in interactive notes mirror the elements you identify while engaging in interactive reading.

Before I leave this topic, however, I want to address in greater depth an issue that may not have been addressed as directly in your courses: when to record quotations.

3.6. Rules for Recording Quotations

Each semester that I have facilitated my seminar, at least one student asks when to use a quotation or when to paraphrase the point or idea. I have devised a set of rules for using quotations. The first rule for recording quotations is to always, always, always record the page number when you are writing out the quotation. I—and most every faculty member who is honest with you—can admit to flipping through articles to find the page number of a quote that plays a central part in our magnum opus. This is not a fun exercise. Please save yourself the trouble and remember to record page numbers fastidiously.

Rule 2 is to type the full quotation into your bibliographic program. In some instances, you type in quotations that you will not use in your dissertation. But many times, with the quotation in an electronic format, you can copy and paste the quotation into your dissertation during the writing stage. Yes, this rule means spending more time now to save time later. Don't worry; the next rule helps to keep you from spending an inordinate amount of time typing quotations.

Rule 3: Record quotations judiciously. Many graduate students rely too heavily on quotations in their introductions or literature reviews. I find it very difficult to follow the arc of the writing when a paper is peppered with quotations. The quotations detract from the writing because they prevent the writing from having a continual flow and unified voice. The vast majority of the time you can do a fine job of translating the author's thoughts into your own words, in your own voice.

Of course, there are times when you need to include a quotation in your work when it represents a primary source. In these instances, you might record longer quotations than usual in your interactive notes. These quotations serve as your primary sources, which you analyze as part of your dissertation, so they provide the evidence for your analysis.

When you capture quotations from the literature, specifically secondary sources, I suggest that you record the quotation only if it adds value that you cannot achieve by relying on your own voice. To assist you in finding that balance for your own writing, the following list identifies situations when using quotations adds value to your work:

- When the author can say what you cannot
- When the quote is catchy or edgy
- When the quote is a definition
- When the quote comes from a nationally recognized organization or expert

A wonderful example of using a quote in the first situation comes from my advisee's dissertation. Chris Kasprisin conducted a study examining a program that supported women college students in the fields of science, technology, engineering, and mathematics. Students in these fields are still mostly Caucasian men from northern European backgrounds. Within this context, there was a national push to recruit and retain more women and underrepresented minorities into the field of engineering. Bill Wulf, the president of the National Academy of Engineering at the time, made this point succinctly when he said, "Every time we approach an engineering problem with a pale, male design team, we may not find the best solution."[12] This quote had impact and was a little edgy, in large part because it was stated by a very well respected White man in engineering. Chris could not paraphrase this quote without losing its impact, so she included it in her dissertation.

Another time to record a quotation is when the author crystallizes a point in an interesting way or relies on a strong or comical metaphor. In the next example, the author applied an old farming adage to criticize the educational system's overreliance on standardized testing. Now I don't know about you, but I know that I could not summarize or paraphrase this statement without it losing its punch:

> As we think about testing policies, we should remember the wisdom in the farmer's comment that weighing a pig every day won't ever make the pig any fatter. Eventually, you have to feed the pig.[13]

Paraphrasing this quotation by stating that educational testing does not bring about improvements in learning just does not have the same impact. If you come across a quotation like this and it supports your point, be sure to record it in your interactive notes.

When an author puts forth a new or better definition in the literature, the definition is usually worth capturing. I find this to be especially true if the author coins a new term or proposes a new definition. For example, I like the concept of *the strength of weak ties* and have used this term in a few of my articles. The term was coined by Mark Granovetter in a 1973 article published in the *American Journal of Sociology*. He defined the strength of weak ties by stating "those to whom we are weakly tied are more likely to move in circles different from our own and will thus have access to information different from that which we receive."[14] Because Granovetter coined this phrase, I quote his definition because it holds more credence than a paraphrase of the definition.

Another reason to include a quotation in your interactive notes is when you want the message to convey the authority of an organization or expert in the field. In these instances, the quotations can be less pithy, edgy, or catchy. The value of using a quotation in these instances comes from the prestige of the organization or expert, especially when the organization or expert presents a call to action. Jill Litt and her colleagues use quotations very effectively in their article, "Advancing Health and Environmental Disease Tracking: A 5-Year Follow-Up Study." They begin their article by quoting two influential reports in the field of public health:

> *The Future of Public Health*, the landmark report published by the Institute of Medicine in 1988, provided the following sobering picture of the nation's environmental public health capacity: "The removal of environmental health authority from public health agencies has led to fragmented responsibility, lack of coordination, and inadequate attention to the public health dimensions of environmental issues."

> In 2000, the Pew Environmental Health Commission at the Johns Hopkins Bloomberg School of Public Health . . . found that there was "no cohesive national strategy to identify environmental hazards, measure population exposures, and track health conditions that may be related to the environment."[15]

By including quotations rather than paragraphing, which they certainly could have done, they allowed the prestige and importance of these reports and organizations to underscore the points communicated in the quotations. Note that including a quotation from a report or legislation does not mean that you agree with or support the point in the quotation. It just means that you thought the quotation would emphasize a statement more than if you had paraphrased the statement.

As a general rule, do not include quotations that are very dense, and that therefore need translation, deconstruction, or explanation. Why have someone else state a point, and then have to restate the point so that it is intelligible to an intelligent audience? Why not just state something once? In these cases, I caution you against falling into the academic trap of thinking the more obtuse, the more erudite. Only obtuse academics believe there is a connection. If, however, a quote comes from an influential source in your field, you might consider using it, obtuse or not.

When you read and take notes on primary sources, you probably will take longer and more extensive notes because quotations from these sources, in a metaphorical sense, will serve as your data. That is, you will present the quotations as evidence, and then analyze, critique, or deconstruct them. Keep in mind that being in the conversation in your field serves as the best classroom. Be alert to how, when, and why your colleagues use quotations.

3.7. Plagiarism and Copyright Infringement

Interactive notes, plagiarism, and copyright infringement are inextricably linked. That is, taking accurate interactive notes prevents you from inadvertently plagiarizing or using copyrighted material without proper permission. Being in the conversation and contributing to the conversation mean being aware of how and when to give credit where credit is due. Academic writing builds on the work of the scholars who went before you. I am sure you have been in a meeting where someone takes credit for the ideas of another. Don't be that person. Rather, take careful notes so that you can properly cite and reference the work of others.

One definition of plagiarism is "the unauthorized use or close imitation of the language and thoughts of another author and the representation of them as one's own original work."[16] If you follow the news, you know that plagiarism shows up in academia, journalism, politics, business, and literature. High-profile cases of plagiarism include fiction writers who model their first novels too closely on the storyline and arc of previously published, yet little-known novels, or prominent historians who rely too heavily on the work of research assistants and never double-check the original sources.

Plagiarism can sidetrack a promising career. Faculty members have been denied appointments and doctoral students have had degrees revoked. Avoid putting yourself in a position where you could be accused of plagiarism.

The latest version of the *MLA Handbook* includes a chapter on plagiarism. The American Psychological Association explains, "The key element of this principle [plagiarism] is that an author does not present the work of another as if it were his or her own. This can extend to ideas as well as written words." These are clear definitions of plagiarism, but how do you actually operationalize plagiarism? If you copy six words in a row from another author, is it plagiarism? What about ten words? When do you know when an idea has become part of common knowledge and when it needs to be referenced? Although I cannot answer these questions for you, I do agree with the American Historical Association's Statement on Standards of Professional Conduct, which provides good advice on preventing plagiarism: "No matter what the context, **the best professional practice for avoiding a charge of plagiarism is always to be explicit, thorough, and generous in acknowledging one's intellectual debts** [bold text in original]."[17]

I would rather not grapple with the technical aspects of identifying plagiarism. My antidote for plagiarism is to prevent it. By taking the time to type useful interactive notes into your bibliographic program, you can give others the appropriate acknowledgment. As you are taking notes, make sure you can distinguish between the instances when you have paraphrased or summarized the author's ideas and when you have copied down a quotation. Take careful notes as you are reading and engaging in prewriting to prevent plagiarism and that horrible, last-minute exercise of flipping through articles or books to find the page number for a particularly pithy quote.

A close cousin of plagiarism is copyright infringement. A definition of copyright infringement is the following:

> Copyright infringement (or copyright violation) is the unauthorized use of material that is covered by copyright law, in a manner that violates one of the copyright owner's exclusive rights, such as the right to reproduce or perform the copyrighted work, or to make derivative works.[18]

The illegal downloading of digital music provides plenty of examples of copyright infringement covered by the mass media. Notice that copyrights are covered by law and therefore can have legal remedies; plagiarism addresses issues of professional standards, and professional sanctions serve as the remedies. As an academic, you build on the work of others. Therefore, avoid plagiarism and honor copyrights.

Earlier in this chapter, in Figure 3.1, I include a reproduction of a screen shot from EndNote, a proprietary software program. The screen shot is covered by copyright laws. Therefore, I had to, and did, obtain copyright permission so that I could use the screen shot in this book. The software company provided me with the exact wording it wanted me to use to acknowledge its copyright, and I included this in the endnote reference I inserted when first discussing EndNote.

3.8. Group Exercises for Interactive Reading and Note Taking

My students and I spend time in class engaging in interactive reading and note taking. I ask my students to bring in a book or a few articles relevant to their work that they have not read. Then, we spend thirty to forty minutes engaging in interactive reading individually. After that time, I ask the group to come together and we share our experiences.

I usually go first and I point out where I underlined or added margin notes on the article. I show them that most of my preliminary notes are near the beginning and the end of the article. Then, we go around the room and everyone shares their experiences. Some of my students comment on the difference between taking notes while reading and waiting to take notes until they complete the reading. We generally agree that reading the whole article before taking notes saves time. Others point out the advantage of reading while looking for particular elements of the article. At least one student per seminar shares that she does not like working in a public area. This point prompts us to talk about our own idiosyncrasies and how we need to honor them (or change them) to suit our goals and work styles.

During this discussion, I emphasize that, although interactive note taking is a technique that I propose, I really want them to embrace the underlying concept. I want them, and you, to be able to make good use of your reading time. I want you to be able to read something once and apply what you have read to your dissertation. I want you to be able to refer back to useful notes when you are organizing and planning your dissertation—not to shuffle through pages of articles or stacks of books. Consider the underlying concept, review the techniques I have presented here for taking useful notes, and modify the techniques so that they work for you. Then share your new techniques with your classmates and e-mail me your suggestions so that I can include them in a future version of this book.

At the next class, I ask my students to bring in multiple copies of their interactive notes. We divide into small groups and discuss the various ways we have customized our interactive notes. As I read through my students' interactive notes, one of the most common phrases I write back to my students is something like "your memory is fickle, be sure to define your terms now." If they have identified an important definition in the article, I suggest that they record the definition as a quotation and remind them to record the page number.

If you are using this book in a formal writing seminar or with a group of classmates, why not take this opportunity to make the reading and note taking process more public? By making these processes public, you get feedback on your work and learn from one another. Share your interactive notes with each other. Can you identify the big picture in the interactive notes? Did your classmate record the theoretical/conceptual approach? How did she record the methodologies? How could your classmate be more precise and concise with her notes? How can you help your classmates to take useful and efficient notes? As you identify shortcuts that can be used in your field, share them with your classmates. Interactive note taking is time consuming in the short term, but time saving in the long term.

Notes

1. K. Anders Ericsson and Neil Charness, "Expert Performance."
2. Tyler Anbinder, "From Famine to Five Points," 353.
3. Ibid., 356.
4. Ibid., 356, 86.
5. The statistical hypothesis consists of writing the null hypothesis (H_0: $u_1 = u_2$), while the research hypothesis consists of presenting the alternative hypothesis (H_1: $u_1 > u_2$).
6. Karen R. Harris, Steve Graham, and Linda H. Mason, "Improving the Writing, Knowledge, and Motivation of Struggling Young Writers," 296, 99.
7. Ibid., 335.
8. H. J. Jackson, *Romantic Readers*.
9. Ken Hyland, *Writing in the Academy*, 17.
10. EndNote screen shots reprinted with the permission of Thomson Corporation. EndNote is a registered trademark of the Thomson Corporation.
11. Wikipedia contributors, "Comparison of Reference Management Software."
12. William A. Wulf, "Diversity in Engineering," 11.
13. Audrey L. Amrein and David C. Berliner, "A Research Report: The Effects of High-Stakes Testing," 37.
14. Mark S. Granovetter, "The Strength of Weak Ties," 1371.
15. Jill S. Litt and others, "Advancing Health and Environmental Disease Tracking," 456.
16. Wikipedia contributors, "Plagiarism," ¶ 1.
17. *MLA Handbook for Writers of Research Papers*, 7th ed.; *Publication Manual for the American Psychological Association*, 5th ed., 349; and American Historical Association, "Statement on Standards of Professional Conduct," under "4. Plagiarism," ¶ 5.
18. Wikipedia contributors, "Copyright Infringement," ¶ 1.

4

CITEABLE NOTES

*Generalizations, abstractions, and theories need particulars, concretes,
and details to support and exemplify them.*

—Robert J. Nash, *Liberating Scholarly Writing*

G REAT QUOTE. When I first share it with my students, they regularly ask how they can keep track of all the "particulars, concretes,
and details" and put them in the appropriate place in their dissertations. *Citeable notes* help you format the main points of the mounds of
reading you have done so that you can use them as you plan and then
write your dissertation. With a useful set of citeable notes, you can insert
the "particulars, concretes, and details" to support the "generalizations,
abstractions, and theories" of your dissertation.

By now, you have engaged in interactive reading and have conversed
with some of the contributors in your field. I hope you took the time to
enter into your bibliographic program interactive notes on articles,
books, monographs, and book chapters. By writing interactive notes, you
record your thoughts about others' work. By taking interactive notes,
you start writing—perhaps before you are ready and before any negative
internal critics are aware that you are engaging in the writing process.

In the illustration of the Single System (review Figure 1.5), you can see
that citeable notes are represented by a few pieces of paper—not the
stacks of paper that symbolize interactive reading or the short stack of

papers that represents interactive notes. By taking citeable notes, you create small pieces of reference materials that you will use to plan, organize, and write your dissertation.

Citeable notes come from your interactive notes and include the "active ingredients" of the article or book. Citeable notes serve several purposes: They facilitate your giving credit where credit is due and prevent plagiarism. They provide small building blocks that you can use to analyze and categorize the literature in your field. And they can be categorized—thematically, by author, chronologically, or geographically—because coding and grouping short phrases is much easier than doing the same with longer notes or with the original reading material. By categorizing the literature, you can plan and write about the literature pertaining to your dissertation topic, which is necessary whether your field requires you to provide a separate chapter for the literature review or to weave the literature throughout your whole dissertation.

In addition, citeable notes serve as tools for adding references to your outlines and then act as placeholders for when you are writing your dissertation. In one of my seminars, we were discussing interactive and citeable notes when one student commented that recording notes takes *a lot* of time. She also commented that taking interactive notes as well as citeable notes seems redundant. I gave her plenty of time to air her concerns, but before I could answer another student jumped in and said, "Yeah, but it saves so much time later on." This second student explained that citeable notes helped her to add references to the outline she had discussed with her dissertation adviser. In the past, she would have stared at her outline and at her stacks of papers but would not have known how to synthesize the two. She said that by referring to her citeable notes, it was a "snap" to add the references to her outline. Similarly, after you outline your dissertation, you can add the appropriate citeable notes to the various sections. By doing so, you can see for which sections you have read enough and for which sections you need to read more.

After you add the citeable notes to your outline, they serve as placeholders. As you write prose, you can refer from your citeable notes to their corresponding interactive notes. As a result, you have a ready system for referencing the literature without having to flip through inordinate numbers of pages. Rather, you pull up the interactive notes you saved on your computer.

Quite simply, here are two examples of citeable notes:

(Single, 2009) Book emphasizes the role of prewriting in academic writing
(Single, 2009) Encourages use of writing groups for dissertation writers

To write citeable notes, first create a unique identifier that represents each interactive note. Sometimes you need to include two authors' last names to create a unique identifier for an interactive note. Sometimes you need to add a letter after the date to distinguish sources written by the same author and published in the same year, such as (Single, 2009a) and (Single, 2009b).

Next, write a very succinct statement of the conclusions or findings as the second part of the citeable note. As a result, often you will have a few citeable notes for each interactive note. The more focused each citeable note is, the more flexibility you have when categorizing your notes. Also write citeable notes for quotations that you may use in your dissertation. You do not need to type out the whole quotation; of course, you could copy and paste the quotation from your interactive notes, but a better idea is to include the point of and a few words from the quote—just enough so that you can readily identify the quote in your interactive notes.

4.1. Recording Citeable Notes and Building Your Literature Review

Your citeable notes come from your interactive notes, not from the original reading. I suggest that you write your citeable notes soon after you have written an interactive note and while the ideas are still fresh in your mind. Typing your citeable notes into your bibliographic program now will make your life easier later.

Choose one field in your bibliographic program in which to enter your citeable notes. I use the Research Notes field in EndNote. Also, I suggest that you type each citeable note on a separate line, which makes it easier for you later when you are coding and categorizing the notes.

Citeable notes will help you play around with, make sense of, and categorize the literature in your field. To do so, you need to be able to print out your citeable notes so that you can readily review and code them. To do this in EndNote, I had to create a style, or format, to use to review my notes. I picked a format that I never use for my own writing, in this case Research Strategies. In Figure 4.1, I circled and identified this style in the screen shot from EndNote. On the Edit Styles Manager menu, I reformatted all the templates in the bibliography. I created a format so that only the Author, Date, and Research Notes fields would be printed out. The author and date represent the unique identifier and are printed on one line. The Research Notes field prints out below them, and I type in my citeable notes so that they are printed one per line.

If you get stuck while creating a style for your citeable notes, search under Modifying Style Templates in the Help index. You can also use Google to search on subjects such as "EndNote modifying style" and find web sites that provide additional information. If you really get stuck, ask

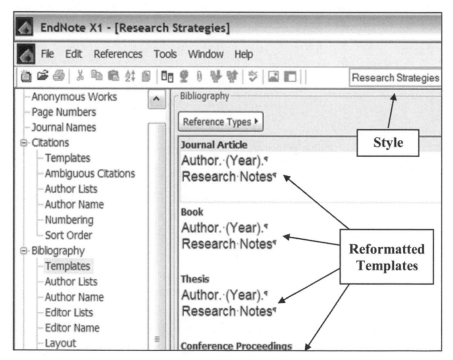

FIGURE 4.1. Creating a Style in EndNote for Citeable Notes

for help from your university's EndNote guru, typically a research librarian. Bring this book with you and show him Figure 4.1 so that he has an idea of the type of style you want to create. The research librarian is a valuable resource, so while you are there, you may want to share with him your dissertation topic and ask for any resources or sources that he may know about.

After reformatting the style, I can print out my citeable notes in a format that helps me to review and categorize them. Figure 4.2 shows the template that I created for the citeable notes printout, along with a template for categorizing them. After you have read a sufficient amount of the literature, written interactive notes, and entered citeable notes, print out the list of your citeable notes using the Research Strategies style. The first step in analyzing citeable notes is to read through them in one sitting. This is one of the rare times when I suggest that you read without having a pen or pencil in hand. The next step is to pick up your pencil, pen, or highlighter; read through your citeable notes again; and code the notes

List of Citeable Notes	Citeable Notes Grouped Thematically
Author #1 (2009) - Citeable Note #1 - Citeable Note #2 - Citeable Note #3	Theme 1 (Author #1): Citeable Note #2 (Author #3): Citeable Note #3
Author #2 (2009) - Citeable Note #1 - Citeable Note #2	Theme 2 (Author #1): Citeable Note #1 (Author #1): Citeable Note #3 (Author #3): Citeable Note #2
Author #3 (2007) - Citeable Note #1 - Citeable Note #2 - Citeable Note #3	Theme 3 (Author #2): Citeable Note #1 (Author #2): Citeable Note #2 (Author #4): Citeable Note #1
Author #4 (2005) - Citeable Note #1	

FIGURE 4.2. Template for Printing and Grouping Citeable Notes

into groups or themes. By coding your citeable notes into groups or themes, you can look at your field and your reading from a very high level. Do not focus on the details, but on the dominant themes and ideas running through the literature.

You can use a few reliable categorization schemes to organize your notes. You can organize them *chronologically*, based on the time period being studied or the date that the research was published. You can organize them *theoretically*, grouping the literature based on the development of a theory or theoretical approach. You can organize them *thematically*, which is probably the most popular categorization scheme. Some other categorization schemes include by *population*, where the study participants are grouped by age, education level, sex, race/ethnicity, or other characteristics; and *geographical* grouping, based on the various regions of a state, nation, or global area.

As you begin coding citeable notes and identifying groups, you will see that you could slice and dice the literature in various ways. If you have not decided on one scheme, you could code according to two different schemes; for example, a theoretical scheme and a chronological scheme. The truth is that writing an overview of the literature is a messy, circular, and dynamic process. Please be patient with yourself and rely on the support and good humor of your writing group as you are organizing your citeable notes.

The process of coding your notes into categories is the first step in contributing to the conversation because you view the literature through your unique lens and organize it into groupings that you identify. This is the beginning of the creative process that leads to your completed dissertation. Mind you, the creative process is not a perfectly efficient process. It requires you to play with ideas, create new connections among ideas, disregard earlier thoughts, and synthesize disparate themes. It can be slow and frustrating and can feel like a waste of time. If this resonates with your experience, you are in good company. Writers throughout the ages have experienced the same frustration. Please be patient with yourself and persist.

4.2. Group Exercises for Creating Citeable Notes and Identifying Categories

As an exercise in your writing group or seminar, have everyone take interactive notes and create citeable notes on the same two articles, and then share their results with the group. Compare group members' citeable notes. How do they differ? How are they the same? What is the essential information that should be recorded in the citeable notes? As a group, identify elements of the interactive notes and examples of citeable notes that are the most useful and most representative of the articles. By completing this exercise, you can learn more from each other than I or anyone else could teach you.

You will be able to see how scholars focus on different aspects of papers based on their own sensibilities, their interests in the field, and their research training. Can you identify why your writing partner emphasized one aspect of a paper and you emphasized another? This may reflect your professional mission and the focus of your dissertation topic.

After this exercise, I suggest that you continue to review each others' interactive notes and corresponding citeable notes, except now using notes on articles and books related to your dissertation topics. You can learn as much by critiquing and providing constructive feedback on the notes of your colleagues as you can learn by developing your own.

In small groups, talk through the preliminary themes you discovered in your notes. Solicit feedback from your writing group members. Perhaps, as they look at your citeable notes, they see a theme that you may have overlooked. They may know of some important literature that you have not included in your reading. Share ideas, share notes, share articles, and share encouragement.

5

FOCUSING ON FOCUS STATEMENTS

A problem well stated is a problem half-resolved.

—C. F. Kettering, U.S. electrical engineer and inventor (1876–1958)

NCREASINGLY, I am convinced that the focus statement phase is the most important phase in the Single System for Academic Writing. The more I work with students, the more I realize that those students who construct a clear, concise, and compelling focus statement are ready to move forward and develop a dissertation. If students have not arrived at this point, they seem to pursue different ideas and methodologies, often in close succession, and never really seem to make progress—certainly not at the rate at which they invest their time.

5.1. Useful Focus Statements Are Clear, Concise, and Compelling

Developing a focus statement is more than an academic exercise. Focus statements are fundamentally important when you decide on and develop any project. For example, when I decide whether to take on a new project, I compare the focus statement of the project with my professional mission. If they align, I am much more likely to embark on that project. If they do not align, I can confidently walk away from the opportunity knowing that I have made a decision wisely and with professional integrity.

In the illustration of the Single System (review Figure 1.5), a page that contains a few sentences represents the focus statement. Items to the left of the focus statement represent the work you have accomplished by reading, entering the conversation, and sorting the conversation into manageable bits that you can discuss in your own voice. Items to the right of the focus statement represent the continuing development of your dissertation, from the all-important one-page outline to the bound dissertation. The focus statement phase moves you one step farther along the continuum of being a consumer of knowledge to being a contributor of knowledge.

You work on a focus statement over time. Rarely have I seen students develop a focus statement early in the semester and then leave it unrevised. The act of developing and revising a focus statement is valuable in itself; this time helps you to solidify your thoughts about your topic, your dissertation, and your future research. The focus statement builds directly on the work you did while taking citeable notes and devising new ways to group the literature.

Following are examples of focus statements:

> I found a sea captain's journal, an example of Spanish colonial literature that had never been translated into English. In this dissertation, I translate and annotate the journal and provide the social and historical context for the journey. (Humanities example: Ph.D. in Spanish literature)

> Why do some graduate students succeed and others don't? Is it due to the student, the department, or both? Using mixed methods, I examine how subject variables and departmental variables influence the adjustment and success of first-year graduate students. The study uses data from surveys and semi-structured interviews of students, graduate directors, and peers and from document reviews of departmental materials. (Social sciences example: Ph.D. in social psychology)

> I want to know why college students violate the alcohol policy by becoming intoxicated beyond control. Can we (student affairs personnel) prevent this? By using a qualitative approach, this research explores reasons students provide for violating the policy, as well as the intrinsic and extrinsic

influences that are associated with the event. (Professional studies example: Ed.D. in education)

A focus statement is a one- to four-sentence statement that summarizes and foreshadows all the research in your dissertation. It must clearly communicate the essence of your dissertation. The focus statement serves as a guiding statement for your whole dissertation, and as such I suggest that you avoid any ambiguity or generalities while developing it. The clearer it is, the more it can serve as a way forward; the vaguer it is, the greater the dangers you will veer off into unwanted territory.

A focus statement must be concise. You need to be able to convey the thesis statement or main point of your dissertation very briefly. Once you have done this, you can discuss the topic readily with your dissertation adviser and committee members. You can quickly grab the attention of your readers and keep your dissertation true to your focus statement.

Finally, a focus statement must be compelling. Your focus statement needs to be compelling to you because you will be spending at least a year of your life working on that one topic. Your focus statement has to be compelling to your audience, however you define your audience, in that it must pique their interest and persuade them to read your dissertation. An effective focus statement is clear, concise, and compelling.

5.2. Elements of a Useful Focus Statement

A focus statement is made up of a few important elements: the issues or research questions; the variables or constructs; the sample, sources, or objects being studied; the time frame; the theory; and the methodology. You should be able to list the categories that are appropriate for your dissertation and check them off against your focus statement.

The issue and research questions address the unanswered questions and concerns that motivate your desire to examine your dissertation topic in greater depth. State the issue broadly so that it engages others who are not in your field. State the issue narrowly so that it is interesting and doable.

You should also include in your focus statement the sample, sources, or objects you are studying. Include in your focus statement whether the sample is women who were the charter members of a political party in a

New England state, young students who are participating in an experiment to test writing enhancement techniques, or Latino migrant workers. Sometimes, the unit of analysis is an organization, for example, beauty parlors that played a central role in the civil rights movement or a corporation that is being restructured. The sources could be literary texts, newspapers, or bank records. Other times, the object you are studying may be works of art.

Depending on your field, your focus statement may include a reference to the theory and methods you use. In some fields, the theory and methods are widely accepted and you do not have much of a choice in choosing among them. In other fields, you must include the theory and methods in your focus statement.

As the first step in developing a useful focus statement, in your writing seminar or group, break into groups of two. One person asks the other a set of questions and takes notes on the answers. Here is a list of questions that will help you draw out the essence and important aspects of your dissertation topic:

- What is your dissertation project about?
- Why are you conducting this dissertation project?
- Why should anyone care about your subject (said in a very supportive tone)? Can you tell me the big point?
- What is the big picture, the context or the conditions that make it important for you to pursue this topic?
- When you are finished with the project, what is the one point that you want to leave with your readers? Which three subpoints do you want to convey to your audience?
- (If appropriate for your field): Which theories or methodologies will you use to research your topic? Why is that the appropriate theory or method?
- What data, sources, texts, or objects are most appropriate for you to work with? Do you have access to them? Do you need to collect them?
- What will be the contribution or implications of your dissertation?
- How does this topic align with your professional mission and career goals?

The notes you receive from your classmate after you answer these questions will be far longer than a useful focus statement is. Nonetheless, the answers represent how you truly think about your topic and whether the topic aligns with your professional mission. Use the notes to experiment with writing and revising a focus statement for your dissertation topic. Typically, your first draft is unfocused and too long. As you play with your focus statement, you will pare it down and get clearer on your dissertation topic.

If you can't talk through the preceding questions, the next best thing is to engage in freewriting while thinking about your focus statement. Write down your ideas on paper. Do not try to edit or fix the grammar. Do not critique your thoughts; just write them down. Afterward, you can review and think about them in a way that is more contained and easier to manage.

Externalizing, that is, talking through your ideas, gets the ideas out of your head and into a forum where you can examine and discuss them. It allows your classmates to point out when you seem to be motivated about your topic and when you don't. The more you can talk through your dissertation topic, the better. The importance of the topic might begin to weigh on you and start to lay the groundwork for writer's block. Do not stare at a blank screen while writing the early drafts of your focus statement. Rather, phone a friend—a friend who can be a sounding board for your thoughts and who can provide you with constructive and encouraging feedback. Keep in mind that a focus statement is a tool to keep you focused on the main purpose and value of your dissertation research. Be patient with yourself while developing a focus statement and it will be time well spent.

A clear, concise, and compelling focus statement not only allows you to think clearly about your dissertation, it also facilitates the sharing of your ideas with others. I encourage you to share your focus statement with anyone who will listen; I want you to solicit the reactions of classmates, friends, family members, and strangers. Hopefully, you pique their interest enough to develop a conversation around your dissertation topic. When you present your focus statement to others, they can provide early and valuable feedback on your dissertation topic.

Sharing allows you to gather different perspectives and ideas about your dissertation. Some of these perspectives you may not find useful, but every now and then these encounters bring about great insights that you may not perceive otherwise. I encourage my students to share their focus statements with anyone who will listen.

When you write your focus statement, make sure you write in the first person. One purpose of the focus statement is to get and keep you focused. Another is to keep you motivated. I don't know about you, but for me writing "In this dissertation I will" or "My study addresses" is much more motivating than writing "The literature will be examined" or "This study will be conducted." You will spend a lot of time concentrating on your dissertation topic. Even if your field favors the passive voice—and fewer fields do—write your focus statement in the first person in the active voice. Give yourself the credit now for all the work that is ahead of you.

5.3. Providing Useful Feedback

Around the time that I begin talking about focus statements with the students in my writing seminar, we are regularly sharing our work with one another. Naturally, we solicit and give feedback and suggestions to one another, so I take some time to set out rules for soliciting and providing useful and supportive feedback.

First, I want to debunk the myth that knowledge moves forward through conflict. That is not the case; although you might have heard of seminars in which students' work is shredded and conferences where a speaker is skewered, these are few and far between. Knowledge moves forward through collegial give and take. Even if conflict is the primary medium for moving forward in a specific field, I do not allow it in my seminar. My students can engage in scholarly conflicts outside the classroom; inside the classroom, we engage in supportive and constructive critiques.

After stating my beliefs about the futility of conflict, I share my wish that we treat each other graciously and kindheartedly. That does not mean that we do not criticize one another; we do, but we give constructive criticism. In my class, we subscribe to what Robert Nash calls "the 'Golden Rule' of seminar conversation: Respond to others in the class the way that you would like them to respond to you."[1]

We have three rules that we follow in class. Rule 1: Surround constructive criticism with encouragement. Anyone who has ever taken management or supervisory training has probably heard of this rule. Whenever we provide feedback to each other, we first point out at least one strength of the interactive note, focus statement, or outline, and then present our question or constructive criticism.

Rule 2: Be more explicit rather than less explicit. Depending on body language and tone of voice with which it is said, people can interpret the phrase "What did you mean by that?" as genuinely inquisitive or highly dismissive. I encourage my students to be precise while framing their questions—the more precise, the less likely that the questions will be misunderstood. Rather than "What did you mean by that?" I suggest questions such as: "I'm intrigued by your theory. What did you mean by using it in that context?" or "I don't quite understand what you mean by [a specific point]. Could you please explain it a little more?"

Rule 3: Own your comments. By owning your comments, you allow the presenter to answer you in a constructive manner. In my class, I do not allow comments such as "That theory doesn't make sense." Rather, we stick to phrases like "I don't understand the theory you are presenting" or "I don't understand why you are focusing on that theory."

I leave you with a another quote from Robert Nash that encapsulates my perspective on giving feedback, a perspective that I hope you too will embrace: "Critique and feedback, when appropriate, ought always to come out of a framework of generosity and compassion, and always with an intention to make the other person look good."[2]

5.4. Group Exercises That Focus on Focus Statements

Regularly, I see students resist writing a focus statement. Most of them state that they are still deciding among various topics. I reassure them that the focus statement they first present will not be their final one. But I also encourage them to put a stake in the ground. At the beginning of the semester, many students have a few different topics of interest. Sooner or later, each student must identify one topic. The act of writing down a focus statement demystifies the decision-making process and frees them to test different ideas with impunity. By experimenting with writing focus statements, students often learn which of their various interests is the most compelling. As mentioned in an earlier chapter, I encourage you to choose a topic that continues to interest you through the inevitable nadir points in the dissertation process. If you must choose among various topics, write a focus statement for each one. This is a structured way to find out which topic engages you more than the others do without wasting too much time in writing prose or outlining.

Make sure your decision is well reasoned, but also make sure that you do not use choosing a topic as a way to procrastinate and sabotage your progress. Because you live within the limitations of three-dimensional space, you cannot pursue all of your interests. Once you make a decision, you will never know if it was the "right" decision, unless you decide that it is. You can experience buyer's remorse, but why? You can always pursue runner-up topics later as a postdoc or in your first academic position.

A final bit of advice: Although it may be tempting to skip this phase, I suggest against it. Writing a focus statement is a technique associated with efficiency and enjoyment. Grappling with topics, focusing on one, and then continually revisiting your focus statement keeps you on track when the temptation to read another book (perhaps not exactly on your topic) or learn another technique threatens to sideline your progress. Sometimes overzealous advisers or committee members suggest ideas that you can incorporate into your dissertation. Although these ideas may be interesting, you want to graduate in a reasonable amount of time. In such instances, having a clear sense of your focus statement and being ready with the phrase: "That's an interesting idea; perhaps I will pursue it after I complete my dissertation" keeps you on track. With a clear, concise, and compelling focus statement, you stay focused as you work on completing your dissertation.

Notes

1. Robert J. Nash, "How September 11, 2001 Transformed My Course on Religious Pluralism, Spirituality, and Education," 3.
2. Nash, "Facing One Another in This Place," 2.

6

TRANSFORMING A FOCUS STATEMENT INTO A ONE-PAGE OUTLINE

An effective piece of writing has a sturdy skeleton. The skeleton connects each part of the writing so that all the parts work, developing and supporting the principal meaning of the draft.

—Donald Murray, *The Craft of Revision*

I F YOU ARE SHAKING your head in dismay over having to write an outline, please hear me out. You may have had bad experiences in high school learning overly rigid ways to write outlines for essays. You may have written outlines, and then disregarded them while cranking out papers. Put all your earlier experiences aside for now. From this moment on, you will create outlines that are dynamic, that facilitate soliciting useful feedback from your adviser, and that serve as the agenda or road map—pick whichever metaphor works for you—when you write prose.

Helping students to transform their focus statements into one-page outlines is my favorite part of the dissertation writing seminar. By this time, I have gotten very close to my students. I have learned about their self-doubts and struggles. We have all laughed about our particular brands of writer's block and ingenious procrastination methods—I often find out that I am not the only one who has a penchant for cleaning the kitchen floor at the expense of writing. And while we share our graphs at the beginning of each class, we have talked about how we are overcoming these self-sabotaging habits so that we can meet our writing goals.

Through the exercise of transforming a focus statement into a one-page outline, many of my students have an *aha* experience. Prior to this stage, their dissertations seem like a nebulous idea. When they expand their focus statements into one-page outlines, their dissertations start to seem real. I can tell when my students have reached this stage. Their confidence and focus increase. I knew all along, but now *they* know that they can complete their dissertations.

The one-page outline is the next step in the diagram of the Single System. The first few stages of the Single System focus on prewriting, those all-important steps of reading, note taking, playing around with ideas, and categorizing notes into themes. When you prewrite, you enter the conversation, engage in writing, establish good writing habits, and strengthen your academic voice.

The focus statement is a pivotal phase in the Single System; it is the phase when you advance from being a consumer of knowledge to being a contributor of knowledge. From the focus statement phase through to your completed dissertation, you develop and refine ideas to contribute to the conversation in your field. As part of the advancement toward your dissertation, you expand your focus statement into a one-page outline, and then expand this outline into a long outline with references.

In this chapter, we will discuss the one-page outline, the role it plays in the development of a doable dissertation, and how you can use the outline to facilitate discussions with your adviser. Then we will examine the various formats of the dissertation, which can differ by field and department. The format you will use for your dissertation drives the format of your one-page outline.

In this chapter, I place the group exercise as the second to last section. For the group exercise, I describe the class sessions in which we help each other transform focus statements into outlines. In the last section of this chapter, I teach you how to use the computer-generated table of contents feature of your word processing program so that you always have an up-to-date outline of your dissertation. As you expand your one-page outline into a long outline with references and then begin writing prose, you can use your computer-generated table of contents to keep track of your progress and to monitor the organization and structure of your dissertation.

6.1. The Role and Elements of the One-Page Outline

When I was in graduate school, a popular bit of advice given to doctoral students did not work well for me. I was told to write my methods section first, and then the results, followed by the introduction and the discussion. Instead, I have found that I work better when I follow the instructions that the king from *Alice's Adventures in Wonderland* offered to the White Rabbit: "Begin at the beginning and go on till you come to the end: then stop."[1] While I was planning my dissertation—and now when I plan any work I am writing—I prefer to organize it from beginning to end. I plan a writing project as a unified whole. During the revision stage, I double back and revisit the earlier sections, but during the planning stage, I begin at the beginning and work through to the end.

The one-page outline is a one-page overview of your whole dissertation. It serves as the "sturdy skeleton" referred to by Donald Murray in this chapter's epigraph. The outline begins with the working title of your dissertation. I encourage you to start using a working title as early as possible; it will help you to visualize your completed dissertation. Right under the working title, you type your name and the date. Next, type your focus statement. Following the focus statement, list your chapter headings, and under each chapter heading jot down a bulleted list of topics to be discussed in that chapter. Do not worry about grammar, syntax, or order; you will address those issues later. For now, just get high-level ideas down on the page.

Along with helping you to view your dissertation as a whole, the one-page outline provides your adviser with an overview of your dissertation so that he can read through your ideas quickly and provide you with useful feedback. The earlier you can get feedback, the better—why spend hours researching, writing, and revising a section only to be told by your adviser that those twenty pages are irrelevant? You save his time and your own by using an outline. When my students bring their one-page outline or other writing samples to discuss with their advisers, they always get more specific and direct feedback than when they go in empty handed. This technique has proven useful to my students whether they are pursuing a dissertation topic based on their professional interests or are working on their adviser's program of research.

Before you review your one-page outline with your dissertation adviser, I suggest that you send an electronic version of the outline to him a day or two before your meeting. Also, bring two copies to the meeting. Some advisers have a chance to look over the electronic version prior to the meeting, some do not. Some print it out, some do not. Some misplace it, some do not. So be prepared. One copy is for your adviser. The second copy is for you so that you can take notes on your adviser's comments. The outline helps to direct the conversation and serves as an agenda for the meeting.

Be sure to type your name, the project title (for example, *One-Page Outline: Demystifying Dissertation Writing*), and the date on the outline. After the meeting, your adviser may put the outline into a stack of papers on his desk. Then, when he shuffles through that stack weeks (or months) later, he can easily identify the outline as yours (remember, he has other advisees and many other responsibilities). Make his job as easy as possible: put your name, the project title, and the date on everything you send him.

Along these same lines, whenever you send an electronic document to your adviser, label it in a manner that makes sense to him, not to you. Whereas on your computer "1PageOutline_080203" may be meaningful to you, it is meaningless to him. Rather, when you send electronic documents include your name and additional information in the document file name, for example, "PegBoyleSingle_1PageOutline."

After my students have followed some of these steps and they share their experiences, they often say things like, "My adviser told me I was reading the right articles, but in the wrong order" or "My multimethods section was too complex, so my adviser suggested I stick with one methodology." One student's adviser looked carefully at her outline and pointed out that she was missing two themes but that otherwise she was on track. She left the meeting having a clear sense of her next steps. Another student's adviser suggested that he use a case study methodology to address his research question. So the student spent the next week reading about case study methodology, and then began implementing it. I have many examples of how students used their outlines to organize the meetings with their advisers, and then came away with useful and specific feedback and suggestions.

Along with helping you to organize your dissertation and facilitating discussions with your adviser, the one-page outline can help you stay engaged during those inevitable times when you cannot work on your dissertation. To prepare for these times, I suggest that you print out a copy of the outline and keep it in your planner or download it onto your PDA. Then, when you have a spare minute or are caught in a boring meeting, you can review your outline. Even if you spend two minutes reading your outline on those days when you cannot work on the dissertation, you minimize the warm-up time needed when you return to work on your dissertation. Additionally, keeping your dissertation outline fresh in your mind facilitates the connections and insights that seem to come out of nowhere but that really are the result of sustained contemplation. In this way, you can stay engaged with your dissertation and use downtime to allow new ideas to percolate.

As you are working on your one-page outline, remember that writing a dissertation is about creativity. Along the way, this creative process can be frustrating; there is no way around it. Other times, creativity can be fun and inspirational. Focus on the inspirational times, which will energize you. Share the frustrating times with your writing group and writing partners.

6.2. Formats for the Dissertation

Before we discuss one-page outlines, we need to discuss the various formats of dissertations and the universal elements that are included in each dissertation. The more clearly you can identify the patterns that are popular in your field, the sooner you can decode the tacit rules about writing. Every field has a template, a formula, a method for planning, for reviewing the literature, for citing sources, for presenting analysis, for writing and revising the dissertation, and for conducting the dissertation defense. Understanding the format or formats that are acceptable in your field is essential to writing a useful one-page outline.

Three formats are widely accepted for humanities and social science dissertations: the thematic dissertation, the data analytic dissertation, and the journal article dissertation. I discuss these three formats broadly and generally. Keep these formats in mind and review the doctoral dissertations that you have signed out from your department or graduate college. Examine the structure and format of the dissertations. The more dissertations that you examine, the more you will realize that your field or department has identified a few formats that are acceptable, formats that you will use when you write your dissertation.

The thematic dissertation is most common in the humanities fields. In the thematic dissertation, the first chapter is the introduction, the last chapter is the conclusion, and the chapters in between focus on various themes pertinent to your dissertation topic. The demonstration of knowledge of the literature is integrated throughout the dissertation. Although extensive literature reviews have been typical, some fields and departments in which published books are an expected part of academic life are moving away from this requirement. Instead, these areas require dissertations that more closely mirror the format of a publishable manuscript, which thereby shortens the time and effort needed to transform a dissertation into a book.[2]

The data analytic dissertation is most common in the social sciences. The first chapter is the introduction, the second is the literature review, the third is the methods chapter, followed by the results chapter, and the fifth and last chapter is for the conclusions. Regardless of the field, there is very little deviation from this format.

The journal article dissertation is becoming increasingly popular in both the social science and humanities fields. Consider this format if you are preparing for a career in which publishing journal articles is required. The first chapter of the journal article dissertation is the introduction (are you seeing a pattern here?), and the next chapter is the literature review. The next two or three chapters include stand-alone manuscripts that can be submitted to peer-reviewed journals as articles, papers, or essays. The final chapter is for conclusions, where you identify and address the themes, conclusions, and implications that span the various manuscripts.

Of course, variations on all these formats exist. Nonetheless, these three formats remain the most popular. In Figure 6.1, you can compare the three formats. Notice that the first and last chapters are the same and the middle chapters differentiate the formats.

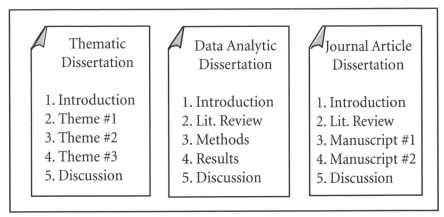

FIGURE 6.1. Comparison of Dissertation Formats

6.3. Group Exercises That Transform Focus Statements Into One-Page Outlines

As I mentioned earlier in this chapter, the classes when we transform focus statements into one-page outlines are always some of my favorite sessions. For the first half of the class, I stand at the whiteboard, suffocated by the low-odor dry erase markers, my hands and fingernails covered with fine black, red, or purple dust. The advanced doctoral student with whom I am co-teaching takes over for the second half of class. I do coach him, but for very good pedagogical reasons I let him take the lead. I want the students to realize that there is nothing magical about my facilitating this process. I want the students to realize that they can facilitate the process for each other.

One student volunteers to go first, and I write his focus statement on the left-hand side of the whiteboard. Next, we go through a four-step process.

Step 1: Gathering Information

I pose a series of questions to this student. But before I do, I tell the class that the creative part of our brain is different from the organizing part. I emphasize that this step is simply data gathering. I ask the student to think out loud and not to worry about wording or order; we are recording his responses on a whiteboard that we can easily erase. When I ask questions, I push the student to be as precise as possible with each answer. The more clearly he can address the questions, the greater clarity he will have when he expands his one-page outline into a long outline with references.

Of course, revise the following questions so that they are applicable to your writing group. The specific questions you use are less important than providing each other with an opportunity to discuss your dissertation topics in a focused manner.

As I ask the questions, I write the student's answers on the whiteboard.

- What will this paper buy you? What is your purpose for writing this dissertation? What will keep you going when you want to give up on the process and go into accounting?
- What is the topic of the dissertation you want to write? What audience do you want to reach and why?
- What is the big point? Why should we care about your topic? What's the big deal? Why should the president of the United States care? The Secretary of the Treasury? The ambassador to China? The director of the NIH? NSF? NEA? MOMA or the AHA?[3] (Pick whichever high-up mucky-muck is pertinent to the student's topic. When answering these questions, sometimes students take for granted that the values they embrace are widely embraced. However, that is not always the case. As a result, I push them to go beyond answers like "because social justice/affirmative action/diversity/gender equity is important" or beyond responding to me with that blank look that tells me that they think I am being racist, sexist, ageist, disablist, homophobic, or just plain daft. I explain to them that they need to be able to explain the importance of their dissertations to an audience who may not hold their assumptions. This exercise forces them to think more broadly about the implications and importance of their dissertation topics.)
- What is the big picture or context for your dissertation topic? What are the demographic, economic, political, social, or academic reasons that make it important to address your dissertation topic? Has a well-known or prestigious author or organization emphasized the need for scholarship on your topic?

- What do we know about your topic? List the three most salient points that are reported in the literature.
- What don't we know? Have scholars pointed this out already?
- How will your dissertation address what we don't know? How will your dissertation force the field to look at your topic in a new way? How will your dissertation debunk widely held beliefs with which you disagree? What will be your contribution?
- What definitions do you need to provide or what terms do you need to operationalize?
- What sources or data will you be using? Do you have them or do you need to obtain or collect the sources/data? Why did you choose these texts/sources/data to address your research questions? What site or sites will you use?
- Which theories or methodologies will you use? How do they relate to your big point and the contribution you will make through your dissertation?
- What do you expect to find? (Students who have generated hypotheses for their dissertations find this question easy to answer. Students who apply a constructivist approach to their research balk at this question. They say something like, "How should I know? I haven't done the research yet," but I push them and we realize that a limited number of results are possible.)
- How will your findings influence the field? How will this new information be applied? What difference will it make?

After we go through this exercise, I look back at the whiteboard and repeat what the student has just stated. I find this important because all I am doing is highlighting the information the student already knows. Then, before we go to the next step, I ask the student and the whole class whether they have additional questions or comments.

Step 2: Bringing Order

Next, I walk over to the large flip chart leaning on the easel. Step 1 is about getting information out and recorded, regardless of order. In step 2, we bring some preliminary order to the process—but not too much. By switching from a whiteboard to flip chart paper, the student can leave the classroom later with a written outline of his dissertation. He does not have to take notes; he can just think and respond.

I ask many of the same questions that I asked earlier, but in a different order and with more clarity. This time I write his answers in an outline format. I write the theme of each chapter as a main heading and the information included in that chapter as a bulleted list below the main heading. If he is writing a thematic dissertation, I ask the student to identify the big picture, the big point and, if applicable, the theory for the introductory chapter. Even before the student has started to conduct his research, I ask him to identify the three most salient themes of his dissertation, which may become the themes for chapters 2–4. These may not be the final themes he uses in his dissertation, but he will have a pretty good sense of the broad themes that are important in his field and for his dissertation. Then, under each theme, I ask him to address what we know about this theme and what we don't know. Then, for chapter 5, the final chapter, I ask the student to make an educated guess about the conclusions and implications of his dissertation.

If he is writing a data analytic dissertation, I have the student identify the big picture and the big point for chapter 1: The Introduction. As part of chapter 2: The Literature Review, I ask him to tell us the three most salient themes he found while organizing his citeable notes. Under each theme for the literature review, I ask him to address what we know about this theme and what we don't know. Next, I ask him questions about his methods and include his answers under chapter 3: Methods. For chapter 4, I ask the student to identify the analytic methods he will use and the possible results from these analyses. If writing a quantitative data analytic dissertation, well before the data are collected, the student can identify the hypotheses, the possible results, and the tables he will use to report descriptive statistics and the results of his analyses. Then, for the final chapter, I ask the student to make an educated guess about the conclusions and implications of his dissertation.

For the journal article dissertation, the process is similar to the process for developing a one-page outline for a data analytic dissertation. Except when we get to chapters 3 and 4, I ask the student to provide a title, a focus statement, and an abbreviated version of the big picture, the big point, hypothesis, methods, and results for each chapter, which will be written as stand-alone manuscripts.

Step 3: Setting Goals

Just as we are winding down the questions and the student thinks he is off the hook, I ask him to set goals. At first I get a puzzled look. And then I point to the heading for the first chapter, and I ask him how many pages he will write for his introduction. Students usually predict anywhere from ten to forty pages. Then I ask him how many pages he expects to write for his next chapter, whether it is the first thematic chapter or the literature review chapter. Then I identify the three main themes of the chapter and ask him to estimate the number of pages for each theme.

We continue this way until we have written the estimated page numbers beside all the chapter titles. Then I step back from the flip chart, look at the outline and then at the student, and say, "You can write a forty-page paper, can't you?" Even though I am addressing this question to the one student, I get a classroom full of nodding heads. I continue this line of questioning for each chapter title. After the fifth time the student has agreed that he can write a forty-page paper, he starts to get it, to really get it.

Step 4: Revising and Organizing

While folding the two pieces of large white paper and handing them to the student, I give him an assignment for the next class period. I ask him to revise his focus statement. Through the process of externalizing his topic, the student has a clearer idea of how he thinks about his topic, so he needs to revise the focus statement to reflect his thinking more accurately. In addition, I ask him to write a focus statement under the chapter titles. Then I ask him to organize the bulleted list under each chapter heading and hand in a revised outline at the next class. As I mentioned earlier, we bifurcate creating and organizing. During the class time, we "create." Now the student goes home and organizes. Through this process, students create a clear, concise, and compelling focus statement and a useful one-page outline.

Foreshadowing

Before we end the class, I foreshadow the next steps that I will introduce through the rest of the semester. When they expand their one-page outlines into long outlines with references, I ask them to be ready to identify three sections under each chapter. Then, just as they wrote a focus statement for each chapter, I will ask them to write a focus statement for each section. Next, I will ask them to review their citeable notes and insert the appropriate citations under the chapters or sections. I tell them that, after this step, they will go through a diagnostic stage to review the organization and structure of their outline. Only then will they begin writing prose—even though they have been writing prose all along, in a very nonthreatening way that prevents them from being sidelined by writer's block and allows them to practice their academic voice.

I suggest that, with your writing group or seminar, you work through the process of transforming a focus statement into a one-page outline. I believe it is essential that everyone has a chance to go through this process. If your group is small, stay together and work through everyone's one-page outline. If your group is large, stay together while working through the first person's outline, and then split up into two smaller groups. One person can facilitate for each group or the person whose focus statement was just transformed into a one-page outline can facilitate for the next person. In my class, we often take two to three sessions to go through everyone's focus statements.

When you have a draft of your one-page outline, you can start to see what Donald Murray meant when he said that "an effective piece of writing has a sturdy skeleton."[4] Your dissertation is a series of papers strung together around a sturdy skeleton. You might also notice that you have already written some of the parts that connect to the skeleton. Perhaps you wrote a paper in an earlier course that you could substitute for a chapter in your thematic dissertation. Or perhaps you already wrote a methods section that you could use as the methods chapter for your data analytic dissertation. This exercise shows you that, although you might not have written a full dissertation, you have written various pieces of it.

The challenge of a dissertation is that it is often the longest and most complex piece of writing and research you have done to date. Starting with a sturdy one-page outline helps keep your writing focused and ensures that all the parts support your focus statement or thesis statement.

Can you do this process alone? Yes. But consider going through this process with a writing group or a writing partner because of the power of externalizing.[5] My students are very articulate and have had lots of experience talking about their ideas. They have had a lot less practice writing about their ideas. By providing them with an opportunity to externalize, I play to my students' strengths. I suggest that you play to yours as well.

6.4. Using the Table of Contents Feature as an Efficiency Tool

At this point in the semester, I introduce my students to the table of contents feature in their word processing program. I use this feature regularly in my writing, especially with long projects like this book or complex articles like a review article. At the beginning of any writing project, one of the first things I do is set up my document so that I can create a computer-generated table of contents. Then, depending on the formatting requirements for the writing project, one of the last things I do when preparing the project for submission is to delete the table of contents.

To be able to generate a table of contents, you need to style the headings and subheadings in your document. By formatting each heading or subheading as Heading 1, Heading 2, Heading 3, and so forth, you can build a table of contents easily. The table of contents identifies the different levels of headings and shows the corresponding page numbers.

The sooner you learn to use the computer-generated table of contents feature, the sooner you can leverage it so that you can keep an up-to-date real-time outline. When you have a method for easily creating an up-to-date outline, you can use the outline as a diagnostic tool to assess the structure and organization of your dissertation, to keep track of your progress, and to facilitate meetings with your adviser or committee members. I introduce the basics of how to use the table of contents feature, and then you can get more information on the Help menu in your word processing program. We will revisit the computer-generated table of contents throughout the rest of this book during our discussions about long outlines, first drafts, and revising.

I have found that doctoral students regularly knot themselves up in a pretzel over the organization of their writing. Because of the computer-generated table of contents, I tell them, "It doesn't matter. You know the topics you need to write about. Write. You can switch topics around later, revise a few transition paragraphs, and you will be all set." All the time that you could waste agonizing over organization you can now invest in constructive outlining and fluent writing.

So the first benefit of using the table of contents feature is that it allows you to delay decisions about organization and structure until a later date. With an accurate and real-time table of contents, you can ensure that you have included the important topics. In addition, you can use the computer-generated table of contents to assess your organization. Reviewing a one- or two-page table of contents (or outline) is more efficient and preferable to reading through pages of text to review your structure and organization.

Another benefit of setting up your table of contents is that it can serve as a measure of your progress. Because the table of contents automatically updates the latest page numbers associated with the chapter titles and section headings, you can assess the progression of your work. You can compare your chapters to the page numbers you estimated for each section and determine how much you have accomplished. You can set goals for yourself regarding the number of pages to write and compare these to your actual progress.

Updating the table of contents while you work can serve as reinforcement, showing you how much you have accomplished and thereby motivating you to accomplish even more. At the end of each work session, I update my table of contents. Every few weeks, I print out an updated table of contents and keep a copy on the side of my desk. For example, as I wrote and then revised each chapter of this book, I checked off the chapters as I completed them. By glancing over at the table of contents, I could readily assess my progress. Because dissertations, like a book, are created over a long time, I suggest that you, too, develop some short-term strategies that reinforce your progress. Regularly updating your table of contents and checking off your progress could serve this purpose well.

When you write your one-page outline and as you continue through to writing prose, I encourage you to use at least two heading levels in the table of contents. The first level is the chapter title and the second is the section heading. If appropriate, you may want to include a third heading level—you may delete this level when you revise your dissertation, but this third level can provide additional direction while you outline and draft your dissertation.

You can be creative with the table of contents feature. For this book, I wanted to be sure that I had an appropriate epigraph for each chapter. Scrolling through the manuscript to check would have been too tedious, so instead I styled my epigraphs as Heading 3 and then created a table of contents that included only the chapter titles and epigraphs so that I could efficiently review them on one page. After I switched them around a bit and found better epigraphs for some of the chapters, I returned to generating a table of contents that included only Headings 1 and 2, the chapter titles and the section titles.

Another benefit of using the table of contents feature in the early stages of your dissertation is that you always have an up-to-date one-page outline. That means you always have a method for soliciting feedback from your dissertation adviser. You can print out your table of contents and bring it with you to every meeting you have with your adviser. If you are giving your adviser individual chapters of your dissertation to read, put the one-page outline on top of the chapter. By including the outline, you provide your adviser with a quick refresher on your project as well as an efficient way to assess your progress. Remember that you are working on one dissertation while your dissertation adviser may be advising numerous students, along with writing his own projects, teaching courses, presenting at conferences, and serving on committees. Make it as easy as possible for your dissertation adviser to provide you with useful feedback and to think you are making great progress. Both of these outcomes will serve you well.

Notes

1. Lewis Carroll, *Alice's Adventures in Wonderland*, 164.

2. If in your field you are expected to publish books and you aspire to an academic career, I suggest that you read William Germano's *From Dissertation to Book* before you finish your dissertation so that you can get a sense of what you need to do to get your dissertation published.

3. National Institutes of Health (NIH); National Science Foundation (NSF); National Endowment for the Arts (NEA); New York Museum of Modern Art (MOMA); American Historical Association (AHA).

4. Donald M. Murray, *The Craft of Revision*, 87.

5. Robert Boice talks about the benefits of externalization and how it relates to an increased understanding of audience in his 1994 book: *How Writers Journey to Comfort and Fluency*.

7

LONG OUTLINE WITH REFERENCES

Learn to think about your manuscript as a collection of separate pieces.

—Eviatar Zerubavel, *The Clockwork Muse*

IN THE ILLUSTRATION of the Single System (review Figure 1.5), the one-page outline precedes the long outline. You transform your one-page outline into a long outline with references that you use as a guide for engaging in a regular writing routine and writing the first draft of your dissertation. By relying on a long outline, you can return to your dissertation day after day, knowing where you ended the previous day and what you will be working on the current day.

Before I get into the nuts and bolts of this chapter, let me provide you with a visual depiction of transforming a one-page outline into a long outline. I developed Figure 7.1 based very loosely on the art work of M. C. Escher. In the figure, the largest diagram represents a one-page outline, with a title and focus statement at the top and five identical but smaller diagrams within that represent the chapters of your dissertation. Each smaller diagram represents a chapter and includes the chapter title, the chapter focus statement, and a list of five topics to be addressed in that chapter. The five smallest diagrams represent the five topics.

You get the idea; you use the same format to organize your dissertation or write a paragraph. You need a focus statement for the first and a topic sentence for the second. Then you need to support the focus statement

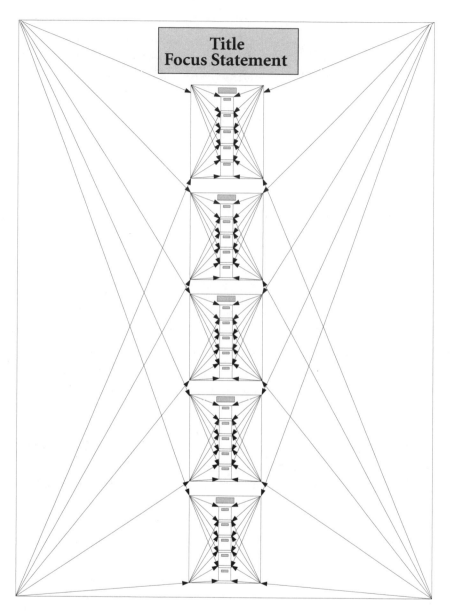

FIGURE 7.1. The Long Outline

and topic sentences, respectively. Although this figure may make the process look neat and tidy, it is not. As you continue conducting your research, analysis, and writing, you will inevitably think differently about your topic and need to revise your organization and content.

7.1. Multiple Purposes of the Long Outline

As with most of the techniques I have presented so far, this technique has multiple purposes. A long outline provides you with a tool for developing an organizationally sound dissertation. The complexity and length of a dissertation make the task of maintaining a solid organization much more difficult than with a shorter paper. The long outline is a tool that simplifies the process of reviewing your organization to assess whether it holds together.

When you write your long outline, I recommend that you start using phrases and sentences. By doing so, you give yourself more practice advancing your academic voice. By writing prose as part of your long outline, you also continue to fool your internal critic into complacency and prevent your particular brand of writer's block from emerging while you develop habits of writing fluency.

Another benefit of developing a long outline is that you can start to imagine that your dissertation is a series of papers strung together. The whole dissertation tells a consistent narrative or story. As part of that narrative, you present original research or analysis. So, yes, the dissertation is longer and more complex than most of the papers you have written so far. Nonetheless, within this long outline framework, the dissertation is a series of papers held together with previewing, reviewing, and transition phrases or paragraphs (which are discussed later in this chapter). Chances are that you have already written papers focused on your dissertation topic as part of your course assignments, so you have already written a few of the "series of papers" that comprise your dissertation. By using the long outline as a guide, you obtain a broad overview of how you can best incorporate those papers into your dissertation.

Just as you did with the one-page outline, you can use the long outline to facilitate meetings with your adviser. As before, e-mail a copy of your long outline to your adviser before your next meeting. In that message, let her know that you will drop off a hard copy in her mailbox. Also, bring two copies of the outline to the meeting and offer one to her if she does not have a copy handy. Her copies could have gotten buried in a stack of papers on her desk or in an overflowing e-mail inbox.

Also, just as you did with your one-page outline, use your long outline as an agenda to organize the meeting. Begin at the beginning and go through to the end. Remember that you may be one of a number of advisees of your adviser. Also remember that she probably has other projects on which she is working. Be prepared to steer the meeting in a manner that meets your needs. If you have something in particular that you want to discuss, make sure you note it on the outline by using the highlight feature or boldface text. Be prepared with some stock phrases to help move the meeting along. For example, if your adviser is overly focused on one section, you can say something like, "You have a good point and I have taken note of it. What do you think of the overall direction of the outline?" Or if your adviser is jumping around and not addressing all the points on which you need advice, be prepared to say something like, "Yes, that is an important point. Perhaps we could go over the outline from the beginning to the end so that we don't skip anything." You get the idea. This is your dissertation and your academic career. Be prepared to direct and steer meetings with your adviser so that you get the information you need to move forward.

During this meeting, use your copy of the outline to take notes based on her suggestions and feedback. When you get back to your office and within the next two days, send an e-mail message to your adviser summarizing the changes you will make. If you already made the changes, send her an updated version of your long outline. Whether you see your adviser regularly or not and whether you have an informal or formal relationship with her, this process seems to work very well. Of course, as with everything I suggest, if you think this plan will not work for you, keep the underlying principle in mind—that is, finding a method for obtaining useful feedback from your adviser on your long outline—and modify this practice so that it suits you and your adviser.

Possibly the most important use of a long outline is in developing a regular writing routine, the details of which I discuss in forthcoming chapters. Every semester I invite a few former students to talk with my current class. I choose students who recently defended, and I ask them to come prepared to discuss the strategies they used to complete their dissertations. This past semester, one of my former students said that the most important practice she learned from my course was the value of writing regularly on her dissertation in moderate-length sessions. She said that having a long outline as a guide made this possible. I commonly hear this from former students.

By relying on a long outline, you will facilitate developing a regular writing routine. Instead of having to think about what you will write at the beginning of each writing session (which is a setup for writer's block), you can look to your long outline as a guide. You minimize your warm-up time and maximize your productivity. You engage your brain to get words down on the page because you have already generated ideas and organized them. If you focus on one aspect of the writing process at a time, you surely increase your writing fluency. If you try to do too many writing tasks at one time or if you try to engage in writing before you are ready, you increase the likelihood of falling into the abyss of writer's block. Make sure you have a clear sense of when you are writing to think or thinking to write, and keep these tasks separate.

A long outline is a tool, not an end in itself. I was in São Paulo recently to give a presentation to a group of doctoral students and postdocs. When I introduced the idea of a long outline, the professor got my attention and added something to the conversation. He asked, "But what about getting stuck while writing the long outline?" He went on to say, "While writing a book with a colleague, I spent so much time working and re-working my outline that I never made any progress on the actual writing. Only when my colleague sent me a few pages of text for me to review was I able to move out of playing around with the outline and write prose."

I always appreciate professors sharing their writing struggles in these meetings and I have a lot of respect for them. It is not a sign of weakness; rather it is a learning experience for his students. Interestingly, I have found that the professors who are willing to share their struggles also seem to be very productive scholars. Too rarely do students get to learn about their professors' writing experiences. Why? I don't think that professors purposefully avoid discussing writing habits; I just think that it doesn't come up because professors and students focus more on discussing scholarship and the research process and less on the writing process.

Okay, back to the story. So I asked him, "Was this your first book?"

and he said yes. Then I asked, "Did you ever share your long outline with anyone?" and after a pause he replied, "No." What had happened was that the project had become so big, so important, so momentous that even the outline had to be perfect. Any time a project becomes bigger than it is, you are at risk of experiencing writer's block, even if you are prewriting. One of the best ways to prevent writer's block and to keep your dissertation in perspective is to share every aspect of the process with others. So make sure to share your long outline with as many people as will listen or look at it.

7.2. Transforming a One-Page Outline Into a Long Outline

By now you have a one-page outline with the working title and focus statement of your dissertation at the top of the page. And if all went as planned, you have received useful feedback from your adviser, which you have already folded into your short outline. You should also have titles for each of your chapters and perhaps a few topics listed in no particular order under each chapter title. Also, I hope that you have taken the time to learn how to use the table of contents feature on your computer and have formatted your chapter titles as Heading 1. When you generate a table of contents now, you get a list of your chapter titles, which is not very useful; but as you expand your outline, this feature becomes increasingly useful.

You will now transform your one-page outline into a long outline with references by following the steps illustrated in Figure 7.2. If you are a pen-and-paper type of person, print out your one-page outline and grab a pen and a pad of paper. If you work better on the computer, open your one-page outline and save it using a new name and today's date formatted as YYMMDD. I discuss the reason for using this date format in chapter 8: Developing a Regular Writing Routine.

Before you do anything, read through your one-page outline. Then, if you haven't already, add focus statements under each chapter title. After you write the focus statements, organize the lists of topics so that they support the chapter focus statements. The lists of topics become the sections in your chapters and style them as Heading 2.

You can guess what comes next. Write a title and focus statement for

Working Title of Your Dissertation
Focus Statement
Your Name

1. Chapter 1 Title
   Chapter 1 Focus Statement ~~~
   ~~~~~~~~~~~~~~~~~~~~~~~~
   ~~~~~~~~~~~~~~~~~~~~~~~~
   - Section 1.A
   - Section 1.B
   - Section 1.C

2. Chapter 2 Title
   Chapter 2 Focus Statement ~~~
   ~~~~~~~~~~~~~~~~~~~~~~~~
   ~~~~~~~~~~~~~~~~~~~~~~~~
   - Section 2.A
   - Section 2.B
   - Section 2.C

3. Chapter 3 Title
   Chapter 3 Focus Statement ~~~
   ~~~~~~~~~~~~~~~~~~~~~~~~
   ~~~~~~~~~~~~~~~~~~~~~~~~
   - Section 3.A

Working Title of Your Dissertation
Focus Statement
Your Name

1. Chapter 1 Title
   Chapter 1 Focus Statement ~~~
   ~~~~~~~~~~~~~~~~~~~~~~~~
   ~~~~~~~~~~~~~~~~~~~~~~~~
   A. Section 1.A Heading
      Section 1.A focus statement~~
      ~~~~~~~~~~~~~~~~~~~~~
      ~~~~~~~~~~~~~~~~~~~~~
      i) Subsection i heading
      ii) Subsection ii heading
      iii) Subsection iii heading
   B. Section 1.B Heading
      Section 1.B focus statement~~
      ~~~~~~~~~~~~~~~~~~~~~
      ~~~~~~~~~~~~~~~~~~~~~
      i) Subsection i heading
      ii) Subsection ii heading
      iii) Subsection iii heading
   C. Section 1.C Heading

Working Title of Your Dissertation
Focus Statement
Your Name

1. Chapter 1 Title
   Chapter 1 Focus Statement ~~~
   ~~~~~~~~~~~~~~~~~~~~~~~~
   ~~~~~~~~~~~~~~~~~~~~~~~~
   A. Section 1.A Heading
      Section 1.A focus statement~~
      ~~~~~~~~~~~~~~~~~~~~~
      ~~~~~~~~~~~~~~~~~~~~~
      i) Subsection i heading
         Citeable Note
         Citeable Note
         Citeable Note
         Citeable Note
      ii) Subsection ii heading
         Citeable Note
         Citeable Note
         Citeable Note
      iii) Subsection iii heading
         Citeable Note
         Citeable Note
         Citeable Note
   B. Section 1.B Heading

FIGURE 7.2. Developing a Long Outline With References

each section and jot down the topics associated with that section; these topics become subsections. As before, do not worry about the order of the topics; just get them down on the page. Then organize the topics under each section and write subsection headings. For your computer-generated table of contents, style the subsection headings as Heading 3. By the time you are finished, your long outline should look something like the middle pane in Figure 7.2, of course, with actual titles, headings, and focus statements.

Theoretically, you could continue in this manner all the way through to the paragraph level, adding headings for each increasingly smaller section. But I suggest that you do not organize beyond Heading 3 because too much planning and organizing can become onerous and inefficient. When you start writing, you will organize within each subsection. You will also realize that some of the sections, subsections, and topics need to be moved around. Plan and organize enough to have a sturdy skeleton, and then let the diagnosing, writing, and revision processes guide you moving forward. Too much planning wastes your time and quashes the creative process.

As mentioned earlier, from the long outline phase onward, you continually diagnose and revise your work. Now is the time. Review your chapters. Do each of the section headings support the focus statement for that chapter? If not, determine whether to revise the focus statement or the section headings so that they align. Review each section. Do the subsection headings support the section focus statement? Likewise, if either needs revision to be congruent, go ahead and revise. Move the order of the topics so that they best support the focus statement.

Although I do not discuss writing prose until chapter 9, I think it is important to introduce an idea now that I discuss in greater depth later. In dissertation writing, whether you start at the chapter, section, or subsection level, each level can contain four, and only four, types of paragraphs: paragraphs that support your focus statements for that chapter or section, that preview forthcoming attractions, that review previous points, or that transition between topics. That is it. The paragraphs that support your focus statements address your dissertation topic; the previewing, reviewing, and transitioning paragraphs hold the dissertation together. Okay, that seems pretty black-and-white, and I presented it that way to make a point. The truth is that sometimes paragraphs include a few of the four elements. So a paragraph that provides evidence to support your focus statement may end with a review sentence or phrase.

The next thing to do is transfer the estimated page lengths from your one-page outline to your long outline. Then estimate the page length of each chapter section and write it on your long outline. This exercise reinforces that you are more than capable of completing your dissertation. Plus, it prepares you for developing and engaging in a regular writing routine.

While you develop your long outline, you must decide how to introduce your topic. I call this choosing which door to walk through; others more commonly refer to this as devising a hook. You can enter your dissertation topic through various doors just as you can walk into a large performance hall or a sports stadium through various doors. The larger and more complex the topic, the more options you have in terms of introducing it. How you introduce your dissertation topic should be influenced by two considerations. The first is based on the current zeitgeist or movements in your field. When I wrote my dissertation under the direction of Bob Boice, I was inclined to enter through the topic of graduate education. Based on his knowledge of the field and because he was solidly in the conversation, he suggested that I start by discussing the importance of the first year of graduate school. I took his suggestion because the way he explained it made a lot of sense to me and it turned out to be very good advice.

The second consideration is based on choosing the door (that is, topic) that resonates with how you view your dissertation work. You are in the conversation, after all, and must have formed some opinions about the conversation. Of course, get your dissertation adviser involved in this discussion so that she can offer suggestions.

The following excerpt from my dissertation titled "Socialization Experiences of New Graduate Students" illustrates how I walked in the door. Notice that I stated the purpose of my dissertation right up front. Although I obtained my degree in social psychology, my dissertation spanned the fields of social psychology, education, and business administration. See what you think:

> If the experiences of graduate students parallel other newcomer experiences, such as those of new faculty, manager trainees, and undergraduates,

the first year may be particularly influential in their socialization and development as academics. Yet we know very little about the experiences of new graduate students because little systematic research has been conducted.

In this paper I try to fill that void: I describe the first-year socialization experiences of graduate students . . .[1]

I led with the idea that the first year was the area of importance to study. Now when I read this abstract, I would make only one change: In the first sentence of the second paragraph, I would strike out the phrase "I try to" and instead would write "In this paper, I fill that void." I put too much work into the dissertation to refer to it as an attempt! Admissions of lack of confidence are all too common in the writing of graduate students and new authors and scholars. These days, my early drafts are still littered with phrases like "I try to," "my goal is," or "I hope to." By the time the writing is published, I manage to strike out most of those wishy-washy statements, although a few do make it through to the printed work wittingly or unwittingly.

I can't emphasize enough the importance of developing your long outline with the support of like-minded classmates or in a seminar. Having the opportunity to talk through the focus statement associated with each chapter helps you realize what you know and how you think about your topic.

7.3. Inserting Citeable Notes Into Your Long Outline

The next step is to add your citeable notes to your long outline. This is a separate step from developing your long outline, purposefully bifurcated, and illustrated in the rightmost pane of Figure 7.2. The more you focus on a single aspect of the creative process at a time, the less likely you are to experience writer's block and the more likely you are to increase your writing fluency. I said that already, didn't I?

Now that your long outline is sufficiently complete, take out your list of citeable notes. Put your pencil or pen down and read through all of your citeable notes and the themes into which you have grouped them. You have done a lot of reading at this point, and you should have a good handle on your field. These citeable notes are the blocks you use to build the case for your dissertation project.

I suspect that you will see a lot of overlap between the sections and subsections of your long outline and the themes that emerge when you review your citeable notes. List the pertinent citeable notes under each chapter, section, or subsection. As before, in this first rendition do not be concerned with the order. After you enter all the citeable notes into affiliated sections, then you review and order them.

Of course, some citeable notes you might not include in your long outline. Put them into a final section of your long outline called Miscellaneous. By keeping your unused citeable notes in the Miscellaneous section, you can review them without having to re-review the whole lot of citeable notes. Also, as you continue developing your dissertation, you may find that you have a place for a miscellaneous citeable note that you did not see at first.

After reading and then adding citeable notes to your long outline, go back and reorganize the citations. The focus statements serve as your compass for completing this step. You may find that you revise your focus statements based on the citeable notes. By the end of these steps, you have a completed long outline with references.

As you review your finished long outline with references, notice a few things. Citeable notes from the same source may end up in various places in your literature review. Good! You originally separated the findings into individual citeable notes so that you could have the most flexibility when inserting them into the long outline.

Also notice that some sections of your long outline include a profusion of citeable notes, while other sections are bare. Based on these differences in concentration, you can decide when you need to continue reading on a particular topic and when you have read enough on a particular topic.

7.4. Planning and Organizing Your Scholarship and Research

Presenting the various theories, methods of analysis, and research methodologies is beyond the scope of this book and would take up bookshelves worth of books. However, suggesting that you include a research plan as part of your long outline with references is certainly within the scope of this book. Depending on the dissertation format that you use, you may include this as the methods chapter, weave it throughout the chapters, or piece it into the methods sections of the chapters that represent stand-alone journal articles.

A detailed research and analysis plan is important because far too many graduate students get lost in their analysis, synthesis, or research; I include myself in this group. We lose track of what we have accomplished, have to rerun analyses or reexamine texts. You can avoid, or at least minimize, these time-wasting activities by having a very detailed and organized plan for the research or scholarship you will employ and by having your committee review and approve the detailed plan. Just as prewriting helps to make the writing and rewriting processes more efficient, a solid research plan makes the analytical process more efficient.

Of course, achieving perfect efficiency is not possible. Albert Einstein once said, "If we knew what we were doing, it would not be called research, would it?" Along those lines, achieving perfect efficiency in conducting research is not possible because you are examining data, a text, source, or philosophical question in a new way and learning something new. Inevitably, what you learn along the way causes you to revise what you have accomplished before and sets you on a different course of analysis afterward. When this happens, I suggest that you document the process and continually update your research plan.

Assign estimated times to each task, estimate any possible expenses associated with the tasks, and predict any foreseeable but unidentified obstacles. Then, as you work on your research and analysis, fill in the results section or sections of your long outline. If you are in the social sciences, you most likely will include a specific chapter for results. If you are in the humanities, you will probably weave results throughout your dissertation. Either way, use your long outline as a tool to help you to keep track of your progress; ensure that you capture the findings and the insights; and prevent you from rerunning, redoing, and rereading what you have before.

Just as citeable notes serve as placeholders that refer you back to the literature, use the same concept of placeholders in your long outline that refer you back to your research results. A placeholder may read something like "present results from ANOVA for treatment 1 here" or "discuss that the dream sequence from x is influenced by dream sequences of y and z."

Even better, write out the results in very rough prose. Just get the thoughts down on paper. You will revise them later. The act of writing out the results of your research or analysis helps you think about them a little more clearly and ensures that you don't lose the brilliant insight into the ether of your memory.

For these reasons, I strongly suggest against the common method of writing the proposal, conducting the research or analysis, and then writing the dissertation. I believe—and this has been borne out in the experiences of my students—writing throughout the whole process is most beneficial. Sure, the amount of time you dedicate to prose changes based on your place in the process. But as you are researching, also write.

7.5. Getting a Format Check by Your Graduate College

Midway through my writing seminar, I hand out the formatting requirements for the dissertations at my university. Although I do not require that my students obtain a preliminary format check, I strongly encourage it. By doing so, my students can avoid struggling to figure out pedantic formatting requirements while scheduling their dissertation defenses and polishing their final drafts. They avoid waiting in the long line that extends through the halls of our administration building during the week when dissertations are due. Rather, by taking care of this check early, my students walk right in and have their document reviewed with little wait.

In addition, from this point forward in the seminar, I require my students to hand in their work with a title page, signature page, preliminary table of contents, and properly formatted margins. I want them to get some of the administrative aspects of completing their dissertation out of the way so that they do not end up typing their title page when they should be taking a few extra hours to revise their final chapter or prepare for their dissertation defense. As soon as you can, I suggest that you obtain the guidelines and learn the formatting standards for your dissertation. Save yourself from having to do mundane reformatting at the time when you should be putting the final touches on your prose.

7.6. A Group Exercise for Sharing and Reviewing Long Outlines With References

We always start each class by sharing our writing graphs with one another. No matter how hokey you may think it is, it is an important practice. By this point in the semester, I have pulled back on my facilitation and usually the students ask one another about their graphs, their progress, and their writing routines. The discussion frequently revolves around when they are able to write. They ask each other about balancing reading the literature, conducting their research, and writing the dissertation. Some have routines of writing in the morning and conducting their research in the afternoon. For others—although I discourage it—the data collection phase is full time until it is completed and writing has to cease during this phase. Students who work full-time often fit in an hour or two after work with longer times on the weekends.

Through the process of asking each other about our writing habits and work weeks, we have the opportunity to reflect on our own writing and working process. We identify the writing schedules that work for us. We learn effective writing and working techniques from one another.

After we share and review our graphs, we break into groups of three based on similarities in dissertation topics. I had asked the students to bring in three copies of their long outlines with references so that they can present the detailed outline to two classmates. A two-person audience adds triangulation in feedback; if both agree on a recommended change, the presenter should seriously consider the change. Students in groups with similar dissertation topics can recommend references and provide more targeted feedback to their group members based on their knowledge of the topics.

About this time in the semester, one of my students typically asks something like: "When will I know when I have read enough? How can I be sure that I haven't missed an important article or two?" "Don't worry about it," I respond. I know that my response is not very satisfying, at least initially. After their reactions transform from incredulity to curiosity, I continue, "If there is a reference that you have missed and it is a 'must cite' in your field, then one of your committee members will let you know."

I do not want you, or my students, to worry about making sure you have read everything and have referenced all the must-cite articles. If you want to complete your dissertation, there comes a point when you need to be able to say enough to the reading. I will tell you, just as I tell my students: "Do not get caught up in reading and reading at the expense of writing and writing."

Insufficient reading is not a common graduate student ailment. Reading at the expense of writing is a more common ailment. With the Single System, you can start trusting yourself and recognizing how much reading you have done. Just look at the rows of books on your bookshelf, drawers of articles in your files, and PDFs saved on your computer. Certainly, you have read plenty by now, so set aside any concerns about not having read enough. Share your long outline with references with the others in your writing group or seminar. They will let you know, based on the number of citeable notes you have written in each section, the topic areas where you still need to read. They will also let you know, in a very gentle and supportive way, that you are banned from reading anything else on the topics that have the highest number of citeable notes.

Notes

1. Peg Boyle, "The Socialization Experiences of New Graduate Students," iii.

8

DEVELOPING A REGULAR
WRITING ROUTINE

*When I worked at Harvard's Writing Center, we joked that the single
most useful piece of equipment for a writer was a bucket of glue. First
you spread some on your chair, and then you sit down.*

—Joan Bolker, *Writing Your Dissertation in Fifteen Minutes a Day*

YOU HAVE TO WRITE a first draft before you can revise it. And you
have to do at least some revising before you can distribute your
dissertation to your adviser and committee members for feedback.
In this chapter, I present some tips for establishing a regular writing routine so that you can get that first draft down on paper.

For most students who read this book, a dissertation is the longest and
most complex piece of writing they have attempted up until this point. If
this is your case and you find this daunting, you are not alone. The goal
of your doctoral program is to challenge you to develop new, highly complex and specialized skills relevant to your field. Your dissertation is the
capstone experience and should reflect what you have learned through
coursework, comprehensive and qualifying examinations, and the many
other experiences you have had in graduate school. Although the task of
writing a dissertation may be challenging, by now I hope that you know
three things: First, that you can complete your dissertation in a timely

manner; second, that you do not have to learn the techniques for success-fully completing your dissertation alone; and third, that you do not have to write your dissertation in isolation.

By all accounts, the first draft is the hardest draft to get down on the page. Revising, which I discuss in an upcoming chapter, is time consum-ing but not as cognitively challenging as is writing the first draft. In this chapter, I discuss some proven tips and techniques for writing the first draft by developing a regular writing routine. I did not learn these tech-niques on my own. I learned them from my dissertation adviser, my many mentors, authors who have written about writing, my colleagues, my students, and my own experience. As with all the suggestions put forth in this book, please try them once. Then think about the underlying principle of the technique and, if necessary, customize the technique so that it applies to your writing style and your writing goals.

8.1.   A Regular Writing Routine

Let us start with the *regular* part of the regular writing routine and by blasting a myth that I have heard far too often from graduate students and even new faculty members. This myth is that writing can occur only in large blocks of time. Hogwash. This belief is self-sabotaging, so let us do away with it quickly. If you write only when you have large blocks of time, too often you can go through a whole workday or week without writing. If you develop a regular writing routine and write for a moderate length of time every workday, you get in much more writing time than if you wait for a large block of free time.

Think of this. How often do you really have an eight-hour stretch of free time? If you did, do you think you could spend your time most productively glued to a computer chair typing away at a keyboard? Proba-bly not. Pretty soon you would get some type of repetitive stress syn-drome. For more evidence to dispel the myth that writing can occur only in large blocks of time, talk with people who hold this belief. Either they are incredibly fortunate and have large blocks of time to spend on writing with few interruptions or competing responsibilities. Or they keep on waiting and waiting for those large blocks of time and rarely get any productive writing done. Most of the people I have spoken with who believe this myth fall into the second category. For every one person for whom this myth works, you will find many more for whom it is a deterrent to their writing productivity.

If you have large blocks of time to write while you are a graduate student, you may also have the same as a postdoctoral candidate. But afterward, whether you pursue an academic career or otherwise, you will not have the luxury of writing only when you have large blocks of time. Now is the time to learn how to be a productive writer and scholar while making good use of the free time you have in between your other responsibilities.

Another myth I'd like to address at this point is the myth of inspiration. Don't get me wrong, inspiration is nice. But waiting to write until you have just the right amount of inspiration most likely means that you are not getting a sufficient amount of writing done. Instead, think of those times when you have had an inspired thought. Chances are it occurred while you were doing something else, like walking the dog or taking a shower. Also, chances are the inspired thought came after a sustained time of being engaged in that subject. So instead of waiting around for that inspired moment to write, start writing to encourage those inspired moments.

Fluent writers write regularly, whether they feel like it or not. Face it. Sometimes you feel like writing; sometimes you don't. Who cares? If you are writing a dissertation and want to earn your doctorate degree in a timely manner, you have to write regardless of whether you want to. Establishing a regular writing routine keeps you moving forward amid other responsibilities and despite your mood.

The first step toward establishing a regular writing routine is to have a realistic assessment of your schedule, and then to block out your writing times before they become crowded out by other tasks. I cannot remember where I heard this quote, but it was from business literature and goes something like "Change plans don't work; change regimens do." In other words, when the best plans are not translated into regular activities they do not bring about any change. You need to translate your writing plans into a writing regimen.[1]

To develop a writing regime, examine your weekly schedule. You probably have a weekly course schedule that delineates your seminars, research responsibilities, and the courses you teach. Block out the times you cannot write, including time for eating and exercising. Make sure you prioritize the events that are important to you, such as picking up your children from school or visiting your grandmother for a weekly dinner. While I was in graduate school, every Thursday my grandmother and I went out for dinner. Because the Depression era remained all too vivid for my grandmother and she insisted on paying, we alternated between having dinner at McDonald's and Burger King. I always made sure that I had a two-for-one coupon to help defray the costs. That time was important to me then, and it is even more important to me now because my grandmother passed on a few years back. Nurture the important people and things in your life while working on your dissertation.

Next, schedule in writing times. When is a good time for you to write? Is there time for you to write every day? If so, mark it on your schedule. If you do your best work in the mornings, spend your morning sessions writing prose or organizing your outlines. Spend your afternoons on tasks that take less cognitive effort. Be stubborn about protecting your writing time. I assure you that many other activities will compete for your time. Some of the competing tasks may be available to you later, some may not. You live in three-dimensional space, so you can do only so much at any one particular time. But for now, one of your highest priorities is completing your dissertation.

Writing is hard work; be realistic. Do not block out eight hours of writing time in one sitting. Overambitious planning only leads to disappointment and blocking. It is better to start small and build up your time as opposed to overscheduling and not meeting your expectations. Writing, like any skill, is not innate but requires regular and continued effort to develop.

Also, do not schedule writing times that are not sustainable. Last week, one of my students came to class with large black circles under her eyes. She had stayed up until three o'clock in the morning writing. She shared with us her progress on finishing a paper with a deadline. We noted that, although her writing session may have been productive, that type of schedule is not sustainable. She agreed and later told us that she was worn out for the next two days. Some dissertation writers can work until early in the morning; most can't. Figure out what works for you and make writing a priority so that you develop productive and sustainable habits.

Next, map your planned writing time onto your graph so that you can compare your scheduled against your actual times. If you plan to write prose for two hours one day and four hours the next, highlight the two-hour mark and the four-hour mark on the respective days. When you have written for the planned amount of time, stop writing. Part of developing a regular writing routine is not only being able to start at an advantageous time, but also to stop at one. Writing well beyond your scheduled writing time only means that you will become backlogged on other projects. And then, as deadlines for the other projects near, working on the other projects crowds out your writing time. Spending moderate and regular amounts of time on all your projects works best. Then you can allocate your time so that you pair your most cognitively intensive tasks with those times when your brain is the sharpest.

Another reason to stop at your planned time is to avoid writer's block. Too often those of us who have experienced writer's block kept on writing when we had the time and the inspiration (and often a deadline). But we kept on writing too long, and then experienced hypomania—which would be okay, except hypomania is often followed by a time of mild exhaustion and depression and results in avoidance of writing[2]—after the up comes the down. I am all too familiar with hypomania because it inspired me through many last-minute writing assignments. When the hypomania was over, the last thing I wanted to do was to sit down and write. I did write again, but only after avoiding writing for a while, and then writing at a frenzied pace as the next deadline loomed. If you too have experienced hypomania while meeting a deadline, you know what I mean. You now have the opportunity to learn new writing habits, ultimately new work habits, which will be beneficial to you as you write your dissertation and then pursue your career.

After a few weeks of keeping track of your writing, put your writing graph and your writing schedule side by side. Examine what is working for you and what is not; try a revised schedule based on what you learn about your writing habits. Share what you have observed with your writing group or a writing partner. They may have other insights for you that promote your writing and the development of a regular writing routine.

By developing a regular writing routine, you also can minimize start-up time, the time that you take to remind yourself about what you have already written and think through what you will write next. Lengthy warm-up times serve as a Petri dish for procrastination and writing anxiety. During those few moments of struggling to figure out where you left off, you may be tempted to think: "Oh wait, I have to prepare for my next lecture," or "Hmm, perhaps I really need to read another article." Don't do it! Don't give yourself the opportunity to avoid writing just because of lengthy warm-up times. Minimize your warm-up time to maximize your efficiency. When you reduce the time lapse between writing sessions, you shorten your warm-up time. The shorter your warm-up time, the more productive each minute is that you spend on your dissertation.

Don't take my word for it. Paul Humpke, a professor of mathematics at St. Olaf College, developed a formula to calculate warm-up time. He found that the "Warm-up time [WUT] necessary to return to a problem increases exponentially with the time that has lapsed [TL] since you last worked on it: WUT = k exp(TL)."[3] I agree. As Paul's formula illustrates, a large time-lag since last working on your dissertation will result in a really long warm-up time. A small amount of time lapsed will end up in a much shorter warm-up time. A shorter warm-up time is always better.

Consequently, lengths of time that previously had been unproductive can now be productive. For instance, if one day you have only twenty minutes to spend on your dissertation and your warm-up time is minimal, you can actually spend those twenty minutes doing something productive. Before developing a regular writing routine, you may have spent those twenty minutes refreshing your memory on what you needed to do and then run out of time before you accomplished anything productive. Before developing a regular writing routine, you might not have tried to be productive in twenty minutes. As you work on and develop your writing habits, you will find that time that you lost in the past you can now make productive.

Sometimes using short sessions to read your long outline is the most productive way you can spend your time. By regularly engaging in your project, you can gain new insights and make new connections during times that you previously considered downtime. For example, some of my best thinking occurs while I walk my dog, read something tangentially related to my writing project, or doodle during a boring presentation. If you are prepared and flexible, you can maximize the amount of time that you spend thinking about, planning, and writing your dissertation.

If you experience a learning disability, be sure to get the support that you need to develop a regular writing routine. Many of the suggestions and strategies I provide can help you organize ideas, manage your time, and persist while working on a long-term project. If you are not already using adaptive technology, please consider doing so now. Dictation software can help you to get your thoughts down on paper and you don't need to worry about spelling or punctuation as you dictate. You may also want to invest in word prediction software that works with your existing spelling checker. For the revision stages, you may do well to find yourself a copy editor and someone who can help to format your dissertation.[4]

Please don't let a learning disability get in your way of earning your doctoral degree. As more people with learning disabilities enter positions of influence in universities and schools, we will be better equipped to help the next generation of students who experience learning disabilities.

8.2. The Importance of a Designated Writing Space

During the first few years of graduate school, you could bet that my desk was always piled high with papers. I never had enough time to accomplish everything I needed to do, let alone to clear off my desk. When I had to work on any of my writing projects, first I had to clear off some work space, not something I looked forward to and one of the reasons I used to postpone starting a paper until it was too late.

Since then, I have learned to maintain a fairly clean desk. I say *fairly clean* to mean that at any time I can sit down and write. On my desk, I have a stack of books on writing, some papers (including my graph), a catalog, my planner opened to today's date, and a set of juggling balls for when my brain needs a break. Intentionally, I do not have Internet access at my home office because I easily get sucked into surfing the web at the expense of writing. The times that I miss an urgent e-mail message are well worth it based on how much writing I get done without the ongoing distraction. I might get Internet access in the future, but only after this book is finished. I find the first time I try to accomplish anything is the hardest, so when I write my second book the temptation to search the web instead of write will be less compelling than it is now.

I know one prolific writer who has a spotless desk with a beautiful view of his backyard and a special rug for his dog to lie on. I know another prolific writer whose desk is overflowing with books, crumbs from day-old snacks, papers, and miscellaneous materials. Some writers go to public spaces to write. A colleague finds writing at the local coffee shop very productive. He sits at the same table every day, puts on ear phones, listens to nondistracting background music, and stays for a few hours to write. Others work in a designated spot at the library.

Designate a spot for writing that you do not have to clear off before every writing session. For many people, using the kitchen table as a writing space is not a good idea, plus your roommates and family members may not appreciate it. Find a spot where you can sit down and immediately start working on your dissertation. Then, at the end of each session, straighten up your writing space. Make it as easy as possible to sit down and get straight to work during your next scheduled or unscheduled writing time.

Prepare your writing space so that you can be the most productive. For example, turn off your cell phone and close your e-mail program (and the chime that notifies you of new messages). Or perhaps you need to set up your electronic posse to give and get support through chat. If you work well with background music, turn it on and get a set of headphones if you need them. If you work well with silence, keep the radio turned off. To maximize your productivity, give your writing your full attention during each session.

In an article titled "Overloaded Circuits: Why Smart People Underperform," Edward Hallowell discusses a condition he terms attention deficit trait (ADT). He describes the core symptoms of ADT as "distractibility, inner frenzy, and impatience. People with ADT have difficulty staying organized, setting priorities, and managing time."[5] Unlike attention deficit disorder, which has both a genetic and an environmental component, ADT is solely brought on by an increasingly frenetic environment. If you are answering e-mail, talking on the cell phone, intermittently grading papers, and trying to get some productive prewriting or writing done, I can assure you that you will not accomplish any task well. Not surprisingly, the symptoms of ADT overlap considerably with the symptoms associated with writer's block; both are self-sabotaging behaviors. Right now your dissertation probably is one of your highest priorities, probably higher than immediately returning that text message or responding to e-mail messages within twenty minutes. Give yourself, your writing, and your writing space the attention that they deserve.

After you have settled on a writing space, make sure you have everything you need at your fingertips. I require my students to buy the latest version of the *Publication Manual of the American Psychological Association*, the style used most commonly in education, my field. I have two copies, one at home, and one at the office, both within arm's reach.[6]

In both locations, I have copies of Webster's dictionaries. The copy I have at home is my all-time favorite dictionary. It is the only small paperback dictionary I have found that includes the Greek and Latin roots of the words as part of the description.[7] Learning the Greek and Latin roots helps the words stick in my brain. I have tried to buy a second copy numerous times at secondhand online and brick and mortar bookstores, but it seems that the others who own this dictionary value it as much as I do, and I have not found another copy. Although most of the time I use an electronic thesaurus, sometimes I like leafing through a thick thesaurus, which I keep within reach.

I also have a copy of Strunk and White's *The Elements of Style*. It is a thin book about all things grammatical. Stephen King swears by Shrunk and White; Anna Quindlen has it on her bookshelf. That is good enough for me. Finally, I have a new book that I found and love: Paul Brian's *Common Errors in English Usage* published by William, James, and Company. It is a straightforward, irreverent, and fun treatise on grammar and word usage.[8]

Being practical and having the correct reference guides within arm's reach of your desk is not enough. Your dissertation is as much an exercise in psychological persistence as it is in intellectual persistence. Put messages around your desk that say to you "I can do this!" While I wrote my dissertation, I typed out the citation for my dissertation and taped it to the edge of my computer monitor. This official reference represented to me my completed dissertation and while I worked on my computer, I could always see the reference. Some of my students post the title page of their dissertations by their computers so that they can see it while writing. Others have created a mock dissertation, with a green faux leather cover and gold lettering, which they keep on their desks. Set up your writing space so that you have everything you need to succeed, whether it serves a practical purpose or motivates you through to completion.

One of my favorite writing books is Stephen King's *On Writing: A Memoir of the Craft.*[9] While talking about his writing space, specifically his desk, Stephen King is really talking about keeping one's writing in perspective, much as I have periodically encouraged you to keep your dissertation in perspective. In *On Writing,* King confesses his alcoholism and substance abuse, and then discusses how he dramatically changed his life, in large part with the help of his wife:

> The last thing I want to tell you in this part is about my desk. For years I dreamed of having the sort of massive oak slab that would dominate a room—no more child's desk in a trailer laundry-closet, no more cramped kneehole in a rented house. In 1981 I got the one I wanted and placed it in the middle of a spacious, skylighted study. . . . For six years I sat behind that desk either drunk or wrecked out of my mind, like a ship's captain in charge of a voyage to nowhere.

He had made it. He was famous. His writing (along with drugs and alcohol) had become central to his life. Many other valuable aspects of his life were being crowded out by what this humungous desk represented. The giant oak desk was a metaphor for when his writing (and life) was out of perspective, and eventually he got a new desk that represented, well, let me have him tell you:

> A year or two after I sobered up, I got rid of that monstrosity and put in a living-room suite where it had been, picking out the pieces and a nice Turkish rug with my wife's help. . . . I got another desk—it's handmade, beautiful, and half the size of the T. rex desk. I put it at the far west end of the office, in a corner under the eave . . . put your desk in the corner, and every time you sit down there to write, remind yourself why it isn't in the middle of the room. Life isn't a support-system for art. It's the other way around.[10]

Please remember that your dissertation is a part of your life; it is not your life. Your dissertation is a stepping stone to the next phase of your career. Very few people make a splash with their dissertations—it is not your magnum opus, it is not the end, it is the beginning. Your dissertation will not set the course for the rest of your career because what you do after your dissertation is as important if not more important. As I stated earlier, your dissertation should be the worst piece of scholarship you ever write. Mind you, I do not want your dissertation to be bad; rather, I want the scholarship that you write in the future to be increasingly better.

As you keep your dissertation in perspective, remember to spend time with those people you love and trust. Make sure you nurture these relationships so that they are around after your dissertation is completed.

8.3. Developing a Writing Network

Fluent writing does not happen in a vacuum but within a network of supportive writers. I hope by now that you have found a group of like-minded students with whom you can meet and discuss your writing experiences. Or I hope that in your writing seminar you have made some connections with your classmates so that you will continue meeting on your own after the seminar is over. In addition to having a group with whom you can share your graph, provide updates, and exchange writing tips, you may want to consider recruiting a writing partner.

When I was in graduate school, I was part of a writing group facilitated by my dissertation adviser and filled with classmates. I had tried and failed to sustain a regular writing routine. I wrote a day or two here and there, but I could not really change habits and engage in a regular and productive writing routine. I figured that I needed a little more external support and accountability, so I asked a member of the writing group, Julie Exline, to be my writing partner. I purposefully chose Julie because she did not struggle with writing the same way that I did, but she also would benefit from having a writing partner. For the two years we worked on our respective dissertations, we called each other every workday morning at 10:00 a.m. Yes, for two years. And yes, every workday. We discussed what we had done the previous day, what we were working on that day, and any obstacles or critical thoughts that were holding us back. We talked through ideas that were not completely formed. I am convinced that this one intervention—more than all the rest—helped me to start writing regularly in a way that would eventually become a habit.

Today you can send text messages instead of calling a writing partner.

You could also e-mail each other, but this does not have the same immediacy or impact that calling and text messaging have. If you need daily support and accountability, or even if you do not need it but suspect that it will help, then as soon as possible recruit a writing partner. Share your goals and set up a time to contact one another. You may find, as I did, that your writing partner eventually becomes one of your closest friends.

About this time in my life, I "recruited" another writing partner. Actually, I rescued this other writing partner from the local dog pound. Felix is a corgi and sheltie mix who is great company for a writer. On those days when I did not want to get out of bed, he would insist that I take him out for a walk. By the time we were done with our walk, I was awake and had spent some time thinking about what I would write that day. Later we would take a walk at noon, which was a good time for a break from writing and a reminder to sit down and eat lunch. While I worked on my dissertation, and now as I write this book, he would curl up under my desk or lie next to my chair. When I needed to externalize, he would listen as I talked through a writing problem or read aloud a portion of my dissertation. Mind you, he didn't look all that enthusiastic about what I was saying or reading, but he listened anyway.

8.4. What a Regular Writing Routine Looks Like in Practice

In this section, I share with you what a daily writing routine looks like. As you will see, it is not rocket science and not much is terribly surprising. Nevertheless, I do not want you to have to learn these writing processes through trial and error, as too many of us have already done. These processes are a compilation of all the advice I have solicited about writing from colleagues, graduate students, and authors. I describe how I implement them. As I have said many times already, please try these writing processes for yourself, consider the underlying principle, and then customize them so that they suit your writing style and writing goals.

When I sit down at my desk in the morning, the first thing I do is open my document and save a new version for that day's writing. (Notice that the first thing I do *not* do is open and respond to my e-mail). I update the date every time I work on the document. For example, for this book I named the document using the following format: DDW_080714.

The first part refers to the name of the project and the second part is the date. I have a long list of versions of this document on my hard drive and have also copied it onto an external hard drive. To sort the versions chronologically, I place the year first (i.e., 08) because many of my projects span at least two years. So when I sort on document name, DDW_081231 is followed by DDW_090101. If I put the year last, all versions created in January would group together regardless of year and January 2009 would not follow December 2008. By saving earlier versions, I can refer back to them and review what I wrote, revised, or cut in previous versions. I can copy a section from a week-old document and paste it into my current document, if for some reason I want to reinstate that section. In addition, if my current version becomes corrupted, I have lost only one day's worth of work.

After I create a new document for the day's writing session, I open my Deletes document. This document serves as the repository for all the prose that I delete from the main document. I do not want to lose what I have already written. Although the contents of this file does appear in earlier versions of the main document, I would have to scan through many files before I found a specific section. By using a Deletes document, I have in one place the latest versions of the words, sentences, paragraphs, and sections that I cut from my main document. By keeping all this information in one place, I save myself a lot of time and frustration. Although I suggest that you refrain from revising while you write your first draft, set up a Deletes file so that it is there for you when you need it. I named the Deletes document for this book DDW_Deletes. I do not keep separate versions of this document by date but, of course, I could.

As an example, my Deletes file came in handy while I was revising this book. My editor suggested that I include examples of focus statements. In an earlier draft, I did include a few examples but then deleted them before sending in my manuscript. If I did not have a Deletes file, I would have had to go through my earlier files, guessing on which date I had deleted the focus statements and probably opening up quite a few before finding the correct version. Instead, I opened my Deletes file and searched for "focus statement." Seven focus statements were listed. So, rather than pulling out my hair, I cut and pasted three of the focus statements into the final manuscript and continued with my revisions.

Let me pass along a tip that I learned the hard way. Always, always make sure that the font you use in the Deletes document is a different color from your main document so that you do not confuse the two. If you don't, you might end up doing a masterful job of editing and adding to your Deletes document instead of your main document. In my Deletes documents, I use a blue font color and in my main documents I use black, and I have not mistakenly spent time editing my Deletes document since I came up with this colorful solution.

The next thing I do is jot down the time that I began writing in the "Comments" section of my graph. I do this so that I can keep track of my writing times and assess when I am starting too late or writing for too long.

I use my long outline with references—not a blank screen—as the starting point for writing a first draft. I type my first draft into a saved version of my long outline, which I had previously typed into my computer and that had already been styled with Headings 1, 2, and 3. I also place a copy of the original outline on a stand that sits to the right of my computer monitor. At the end of each writing session, I check off the chapters and sections that I have completed so that the outline on my desk is up-to-date and so that I can identify the next sections I will work on. So perhaps one day I plan to write the first draft from chapter 2, section 3 through chapter 2, section 7. Although I do not always accomplish all the writing that I plan to do, at least this method helps me to keep moving forward.

After opening today's version of my writing document and reviewing my long outline, I conduct a search on "***." At the end of yesterday's writing session, I typed in the three asterisks at the end of what I had written. I am usually very tempted to start reading and revising from the beginning of my document. When I used to do that, my first few pages or sections were perfect and the quality of the paper deteriorated with length. With a mechanism that allows me to return easily to where I stopped writing the day before, I can prevent any temptation to revise before I finish writing the first draft.

At the end of the previous day's writing session and before typing in the three asterisks to serve as a placeholder, I wrote a few notes to myself. I typed in any thoughts that I wanted to remember but did not have the time to transform into prose. By doing so, I minimize my warm-up time at the beginning of my next writing session. The next writing session starts with my reading a paragraph or two of the writing I finished the session before. In addition, I review the notes that I wrote at the end of the previous writing session.

As I begin writing, I make sure that I do not try to write it right the first time. I also remind myself that the paragraph, and not the sentence and certainly not the word, is the main unit of my writing. As I write my first draft, when I cannot find a word that fits properly, I do not agonize over it and search a thesaurus. Rather, I type *blank* and continue on with the sentence. I replace *blank* with the appropriate word when I revise. I use the same term every time so I can search for *blank* and catch any that slipped by me during an earlier revision process.

Likewise, I do not agonize over the structure of sentences at this point. Have you ever struggled to get the introductory sentence and the introductory paragraph just right? I know I have, and I have worked with many graduate students who have the same struggle. While I am writing the first draft, I do not stumble over writing opening paragraphs and transitions. Sometimes I write them and other times I put in a placeholder by typing something like "Introductory paragraph goes here." You may also want to set the transition paragraphs aside for now and type in "Add a transition here" or "Review and then preview this chapter." You can write these paragraphs later while you are revising.

In the first draft, the most important focus is the content of the writing, not the style of the writing. When I get stuck writing content, I type a section that starts with "What am I trying to say here?" And then I answer that question while typing, without the pressure of having to say it perfectly the first time. Oftentimes, I speak out loud and dictate to myself what I want to write. Like many people, I do not question my ability to communicate verbally as much as I do my writing ability. So by dictating to myself I continue writing rather than getting hung up on using the right word. My first drafts are very informal and colloquial, which is okay for now.

When I find that I am really stuck, I call my husband or a friend and ask to talk through a section. I know that when I get stuck it means that I need to engage in more prewriting because I am writing prose before I am ready. The other times I get stuck is when I start to elevate my writing beyond its true importance. At all costs I avoid staring at a blank screen. When this happens, I get up and do the laundry (I mostly work at my home office) and remind myself that life is full of the mundane. I also remind myself that this draft does not have to be perfect; actually my first draft should be far from perfect. Then, when I come back to my desk after such a short break, I do not place my hands on the keyboard; rather, I pick up a pencil and grab a pad of paper and I try again, starting with "What am I trying to say here?" Through this process, I can usually determine what I am trying to say. Or if I am not sure of what I am trying to say, I can determine the type of prewriting I need to do before I can continue writing.

During my scheduled writing times, I mark the sections where I need to do more prewriting with a unique placeholder (such as ### or @@@), and I continue writing. To save myself from having to reassess the type of prewriting I need to do, I place a to-do list at the beginning of each of my documents. In the to-do list, I describe the prewriting tasks that I need to do that match the unique placeholders in the draft. By keeping a to-do list, I can remember my prewriting tasks without breaking up my writing time. If I have to do more prewriting, I will, but not during prime writing time.

I put the to-do list at the beginning of the document because when I put the list at the end of the document or in a separate document, I often forget to review it. Now, I review the list every time I open my document. Often, I copy a few items from my to-do list onto my daily planner. Then I work on the items after my writing time is over. Whenever I have taken care of a to-do item, I delete it from the list.

I do whatever it takes to keep moving forward while writing my first draft. For me, the trick is not to get bogged down in writer's block. Staring at a blank screen is more harmful than just the wasted time—it saps my confidence and I start to question my ability to write. My internal critic notices that I am staring at a blank screen and it starts repeating all those self-defeating thoughts that I have been trying so hard to quiet. My internal critic is pretty persistent and I am much better off not awakening him rather than trying to shut him up once he starts. But writing blocks do occur and I discuss them in greater depth in the next chapter.

As I write, I check off each section I have completed on the printed copy of my long outline (the computer-generated table of contents). Near the end of my writing session and as I referred to earlier, I write a short note to myself that will jog my memory and reduce the warm-up time I need to move into productive writing during the next session. Then I update my writing graph and write a comment to myself about what I accomplished that day.

How do you know when to stop? You can use time or tasks as indicators. For example, my writing sessions are time based. Often I need to stop based on a scheduled meeting or work I need to do on one of my grants. I schedule a few hours of writing, and then stop at a designated time. On the other hand, when a close friend was writing her dissertation, she chose to schedule her writing sessions around tasks. She was working full-time, so it was very important for her to work on her dissertation in short but daily intervals. She began working on the parts of her dissertation that seemed fun or easy to her; often these tasks were closed-ended, such as reading and taking notes on one article, writing up one idea or section, typing the forms that go at the beginning of the dissertation, setting up a portion of her survey online, or analyzing one piece of her survey data. When she completed that task, she put her dissertation away until the next day. By completing the fun or easy tasks, she gained momentum that kept her moving forward while she worked on the more challenging and less enjoyable aspects of her dissertation.

If you are struggling to begin work on your dissertation, I suggest that you start with a task-based approach. Identify tasks that are least likely to trigger writer's block. How about typing the title page and signature pages for your dissertation? Then identify one or two sections from your long outline and write them; skip the introductions for now.

When you have a fifteen- or twenty-minute writing session scheduled and you use a task-based approach, you know where to start and when to stop. You can experience a sense of accomplishment when you complete a few of the tasks. Be sure that the tasks are small and manageable so that you can accomplish them successfully.

As my students develop their regular writing routines, they often switch to using a time-based writing schedule. As you are beginning to develop a regular writing routine, experiment with using a task-based approach and then a time-based approach. Jot notes on your writing graph about your experiences with both approaches. Share your experiences with your writing partners and writing group. As you talk through your experiences, reflect on what works for you and play to your strengths.

As you write, do whatever it takes to make progress. For instance, I happen to love alliteration and include as much as I can in my first drafts. In an earlier version of this book, I have a section called "Peg's perfectly poignant pointers on prose." You might have noticed that that section heading no longer exists. But while I was writing the first draft, I got a kick out of the alliteration and it helped me to continue writing.

Another technique I use in my first drafts is numbering. First, I do not worry about fancy prose. Second, I list ideas on the page. Third, my early drafts often include paragraphs where every sentence is numbered. Fourth, I delete the numbering when I revise. This paragraph is a good example of how I use numbering. You may have noticed that few, if any, of my numbered paragraphs made it through to the final draft. The information in the paragraphs stays the same, but the transitions become less rigid and more interesting—at least that is my goal.

When I am sitting at my writing desk and Felix is snoring under my desk, I rely on alliteration and numbering to keep my writing fluent. If standing on my head would help my writing, I would do it. If you are fretting over a word, type *blank*; if alliteration makes you happy, include it in your writing. If having a snoozing dog nearby keeps you motivated, buy him a cushy bed and place it under your desk. While you are writing, do whatever it takes to get your first draft down on the page.

Well, *whatever it takes* with exceptions. The purpose of prewriting, organizing, and lowering your standards to write is to alleviate stress and anxiety and other negative feelings associated with writing. Nonetheless, after prewriting, organizing, and lowering your standards, you still may experience inordinate stress or anxiety. Do not do whatever it takes, if whatever it takes means turning to excessive drinking, overeating, under-eating, or relying on prescription or illegal drugs to help with your writing. If you find yourself in this position, know that you are not alone. You are not the first graduate student driven to drink by the dissertation and you will not be the last. But do know that untreated (yet very treatable) mental health problems are a significant predictor of graduate student attrition.[11] If you find that you resort to self-defeating behaviors to get through your doctoral program, get help sooner rather than later. Visit the counseling center. If you are not comfortable visiting the center, call the center to get recommendations for community-based therapists or support groups. Ask your primary care provider for help or referrals.

Do not let undue stress, anxiety, or mental health problems interfere with your academic goals, your health, and your life.

While working on your dissertation, you have to engage in research activities and writing activities. Common advice is that dissertation writers should work on their prospectus, complete their research, and then write their dissertation. As I mentioned before, I completely disagree with this advice. I have known too many doctoral students and too many new faculty members who engage in research at the expense of writing.

If the tasks associated with your research plan are more cognitively taxing, work on those in the morning, and then write in the afternoon. However, more often than not, doctoral students do better when they spend their morning hours writing and their afternoons on the research and analytical aspects of their dissertations. Sometimes you must focus solely on your research, such as when you are overseas examining primary sources or you have a set, restricted time for observing participants. During those times, do what you need to do. When you have more flexibility with your time, balance your time between writing and researching. You have to be creative about working around your responsibilities. Regularly review your weekly work schedule in lieu of your writing graph and develop a writing regimen that works for you.

Remember that while you write your first draft, no revision is allowed. You will have plenty of opportunities to revise later. Plus, you need a solid first draft to have something to revise. Keep in mind that the goal of developing a regular writing routine is to develop work habits that enhance efficiency and that you can sustain over time. If you schedule writing sessions that are too brief, you will spend most of your time starting your computer and warming up. If you write in excessively long sessions, you will have a diminishing return on investment, be at risk of developing a repetitive stress injury, and experience hypomania that only leads to writing aversion. Schedule your writing and write in moderate and regular sessions.

When you learn habits of fluent writing, you not only increase your writing productivity, you also increase your writing confidence. Productivity and increased confidence sustain your regular writing routine. In the early stages of the Single System, you honed your writing skills in a nonthreatening manner while writing interactive notes and citeable notes. You found and exercised your voice by including sentences and phrases in your long outline. With the long outline with references, you can spend anywhere from a few minutes to a few hours working on your dissertation because you can pick up where you left off and minimize warm-up time. Engaging in a regular writing routine results in continual productivity and increased confidence.

8.5. Group Exercises for Establishing a Regular Writing Routine

As you transition from the prewriting to the writing stage of your dissertation, I hope that you continue to meet with your writing group. Continue to share your graphs and discuss your experiences with writing. Also share your long outline to show the sections you have completed and the number of pages you have written.

If you have recruited a writing partner or two—and I hope that you have—share your graphs and long outline with them. If you cannot meet face-to-face, you can send a scanned version of your graph or an electronic version of your long outline via e-mail so that your writing partners can review them when you provide an update. You may not want to do this every day, but perhaps once a week.

As you transition to engaging in more writing, set some time aside for a writing workshop. For example, one spring break a few of us got together in a university seminar room. We brought our laptops and writing projects. We started the day by sharing what we were working on and what our goals were. Peer pressure kept us in our seats for a few hours every morning. When we got stuck, we were able to talk through our problem right then, solve it, and continue with our writing. Although you may not be able to do this type of writing workshop regularly, it can be very helpful every now and then. Recruit writing partners for a week-long writing workshop over the summer to keep your momentum going and prevent that experience of "falling off a cliff" that occurs when courses and the other external structures around your doctoral program are completed.

Finally, talk with everyone you know who is a writer and ask them about their writing experiences. Read books on writing. I mention a few throughout this book and provide full references in the bibliography.

Share the books you really like with your writing group. If you come across a bit of advice that you find particularly helpful, please e-mail it to me and I may be able to include it in a future edition of this book.

Notes

1. If you are reading this endnote, perhaps you have noticed that I broke my own rule. While writing about rules for quotations, I suggested that you do not cite a quote that needs an explanation; then a few chapters later I cite a quote and annotate it. Hmm, maybe the larger lesson is that one rule trumps all other rules: The Rule of Exceptions.

2. Robert Boice, *How Writers Journey to Comfort and Fluency.*

3. J. Fleron and others, "Keeping Your Research Alive," quoted in Richard M. Reis, *Tomorrow's Professor,* 250.

4. Suggestions for supporting doctoral students with learning disabilities came from the members of the Disabled Student Services in Higher Education listserv (DSSHE-L@listserv.buffalo.edu). To search the archives or to sign up for the listserv, go to http://listserv.acsu.buffalo.edu/archives/dsshe 1.html.

5. Edward M. Hallowell, "Overloaded Circuits," 1.

6. *Publication Manual of the American Psychological Association,* 5th ed.

7. *Webster's New World College Dictionary,* 2nd ed.

8. Paul Brians, *Common Errors in English Usage*; William Strunk, Jr., and E. B. White, *The Elements of Style,* 3rd ed.

9. Stephen King, *On Writing: A Memoir of the Craft.*

10. Ibid., 100–01.

11. A. L. Turner and T. R. Berry, "Counseling Center Contributions to Student Retention and Graduation,"; S. B. Wilson, T. W. Mason, and M. J. M. Ewing, "Evaluating the Impact of Receiving University-Based Counseling Services on Student Retention."

9

OVERCOMING WRITER'S BLOCK

Lower your standards until you are able to write. Create, then criticize.

—Donald Murray, *The Craft of Revision*

THE EPILOGUE for the first chapter of this book states: *Blocking occurs when writers write before they are ready.* Writers block when they try to create and criticize or write without adequate prewriting. Dissertation writers experience blocking when they try to write prose without having a clear sense of what they want to say or the organizational scheme in which they want to say it.

Grandiosity also triggers writer's block. I find that grandiosity does not refer to you but to how you view your dissertation. Is it going to be your magnum opus? Will it make a splash in your field? Perhaps, but probably not. Striving to write the great American novel is one way to ensure that you will never finish the story. Don't write the greatest (fill in your field) dissertation; write a good dissertation that moves you forward to the next stage of your career.

You also may experience blocking if you are pursuing a dissertation topic that exposes weaknesses or airs the dirty laundry of a group with which you affiliate. I have heard this concern from minority graduate students and graduate students who were raised in low-income settings. Although the information you are examining in your dissertation may be well known in certain circles, opening the information to a wider audience may cause the voices of the past, present, and future to question your reasons for pursuing that dissertation topic and raise issues of betrayal. You may be concerned that you will expose secrets in a setting (i.e., higher education) where we are still striving to level the playing field.

The results? You postpone writing and spend your time on research activities. You agree to submit chapters of your dissertation to your adviser on certain dates and you repeatedly miss those deadlines. You spend time preparing for your courses rather than writing. Ultimately, you may be at risk for remaining ABD (All But Dissertation).

Do not let writer's block hold you back. You can overcome writer's block. In this chapter, I discuss some of the most common forms of writer's block experienced by dissertation writers. But the focus of this chapter is not on diagnosing and understanding writer's block, rather the focus is on overcoming it and transforming yourself into a fluent writer. If you do not experience writer's block, you can skip this chapter or skim through it to pick up a technique or two to support your regular writing routine.

9.1. Perfectionism

Perfectionism[1] is a particularly popular cause of writer's block for doctoral students. My students have histories of excelling in school. They have had their share of A+'s on papers and transcripts. These perfectionist traits served them well as undergraduates and even as master's students. While working on their dissertations, however, these traits are working against them.

Perfectionists edit while they write their first drafts. They agonize over the introductory paragraph so that the quality of their writing diminishes as the length increases. They rarely share early drafts and get feedback only on highly polished writing. They worry about missing a particular reference and so continue reading and taking notes well after they have combed the literature.

If you tend toward perfectionism and it hinders your performance, you can employ specific techniques to transform it from a liability into an asset. Perfectionists are likely to fall into the trap of reading at the expense of writing—you can always find one more book or article to read. Your long outline with references is the tool with which you determine whether you have read enough and convince yourself that you know the literature in your field. Review your long outline to assess whether you have plenty of citeable notes in each section. Share your long outline with your writing group and ask them if they think you need to read more in any specific area or if you are ready to write. Chances are they will determine that you are ready to write. If you don't believe me, at least believe them.

When you begin writing, never ever write your introductory paragraphs in your first draft. Of course you can write convincing and eloquent introductory paragraphs, but your dissertation committee will not sign off on a few perfect paragraphs. If you struggle with perfectionism, take some advice from the previous chapter and use a few placeholder phrases to remind yourself where to insert introductory paragraphs and transitions. As you write, do not spell check. If possible, turn off the feature that checks your spelling as you write. Finally, be ready to use *blank* as a placeholder when you cannot come up with the perfect word. Your goal is to keep on writing rather than to get bogged down on one word, sentence, or paragraph.

In *Bird by Bird*, Anne Lamott talks about the "shitty first draft." She says "All good writers write them. This is how they end up with good second drafts and terrific third drafts."[2] Have you ever seen anyone else's crummy first draft (I hope you don't mind if I use *crummy* instead)? You will be surprised at how bad it is. Have you ever shared one of yours? Does the thought of doing this make you anxious? Do it anyway. If you are a perfectionist, chances are you have not shared a crummy first draft or that you have misrepresented a third draft as a first draft. If you choose wisely, I assure you that the person with whom you share your crummy first draft will not think you are inadequate. Rather, they will be able to give you valuable content and organizational feedback before you have wasted too much time on unearthing the right word or perfecting the sentence structure.

Perfectionists in particular are susceptible to stumbling over the first draft. What can I say? Get the first draft down on paper, and then, and only then, begin crafting your eloquent introductory paragraphs. After you have written a crummy first draft, you can leverage your perfectionism and polish your crummy first draft into an exceptional, completed dissertation. But—and it is an important *but*—you may want to set an external deadline with your dissertation adviser, writing partners, or writing group so that you have an incentive to put an end to the polishing.

9.2. Procrastination

Procrastination is another cause of writer's block that seems to ail doctoral students. If you do procrastinate, you probably have experienced your share of all-nighters. You put off writing until it is too late, and then you use the upcoming deadline to fuel a writing spree. Although this system may have gotten you through your master's program, it will not help you complete a defendable dissertation. If you procrastinate (I can sympathize because this was my most common form of writer's block), your biggest challenge is getting your bum down on the chair and your hands on the keyboard. Once you get over that initial anxiety and begin writing, you usually can make very good progress.

One of the most effective techniques you can use is to recruit a writing partner. In the previous chapter, I mentioned that I recruited a writing partner who seemed to have different writing struggles than I did. That strategy worked well for me. Think about a classmate who would be a good writing partner for you. Have two or three alternatives because your first choice may not recognize a need for contracting with a fellow writer.

After you have recruited a writing partner, contact her every scheduled writing day. Yes, *every* day. When you contact your writing partner, tell her the tasks you will be working on that day and how yesterday went. Contact her via phone or using instant messages; real-time communications seem to work better than asynchronous communications like e-mail. Depending on whether you use a task-based or a time-based approach to writing, keep track of the tasks you have accomplished and the time you have spent writing to share with your writing partner the next day. I know you may be tempted to, but do not misrepresent your progress to your writing partner. In the end, the truth prevails about your writing progress. If the thought of having to be honest with a writing partner is aversive, I can assure you that you will feel much worse when the rest of your cohort has defended their dissertations and you are still ABD.

Another very effective technique is to coordinate a writing workshop with a few classmates. Go to a seminar room, a coffee shop, the library, someone's home, or any place where you all can work comfortably on your laptops while resisting the temptations of procrastination. Just the act of writing together can create the type of peer pressure that helps you stay glued to your chair.

Begin each day of the writing workshop just as you would with a remote writing partner. Name your goals for that day, whether task-based or time-based. At the end of the writing session, reflect on what you accomplished along with what you identified about your writing style. If you cannot do this every day, then try to meet with the group for two or three days every week. A writing workshop often cannot be sustained, but it is a good way to kick-start writing fluency.

I advise holding writing workshops in locations without Internet access. Because such places are becoming increasingly difficult to find, at least make sure one of your writing partners can see your screen to deter you from checking the weather in Dubai or looking up the fuel efficiency of the latest hybrid car. If the Internet is a time sink for you, cancel your Internet connection. If you get sucked into watching the twenty-four-hour shopping network, cancel your cable subscription. Although this may at first seem silly, after you have finished your dissertation, you will have plenty of time to find obscure web sites and shop for the latest electronics. The time you save by eliminating such temptations more than covers the added time it takes for you to travel to your university or local library to access the Internet. If you have a PDA on which you can receive your e-mail, the inconvenience will be minimal. Just have some tools on hand to make sure that you do not surf the web on your PDA after your Internet connection is disabled.

If you are pursuing a doctoral degree online and need Internet access at home, recruiting a writing group or partner who can keep you accountable is all the more important. The chance of running into your adviser in the hallway or meeting a classmate in a local coffee shop is minimal. These types of chance meetings can help to motivate writers who are tempted to procrastinate; you do not have the same luxury. You have complete control over when you check your e-mail or the cohort's online bulletin board and you can readily avoid it with impunity. Recruit one or two of your classmates to serve as online writing partners and keep in contact via texting (for your regular updates) and e-mail (to exchange outlines and early drafts).

Because the struggle for procrastinators is to sit down and get started, it is particularly important for you to have a designated writing space that you keep relatively clear. Anything that makes sitting down even slightly aversive will make cleaning the kitchen floor all the more enticing. Any distractions on the desk provide you with a ready reason to delay writing. Find or create a designated writing space and stick to using it. This space may be in your home, in your office, or at the local coffee shop.

As I mentioned earlier, your challenge is to get started. Sometimes sitting down at your desk is not enough. Although you have your long outline with references and external supports such as writing partners and a writing group on hand, sometimes you still get stuck. An effective way to get unstuck before succumbing to the temptation of procrastination is to journal. Sit down at your desk, turn on your computer, and open the document on which you will be working. Then pull out a pad of paper and a pencil or pen and begin journaling about the work you plan to do that day. For the two years that I worked on my dissertation, I journaled almost every day. I would start by writing, "Okay, I am feeling like I am blocking and I do not know what to say . . . " and after half a page or so of that, I would write, "What I want to write about today is . . ." I almost always ended my journal entry with, "Okay, that sounds good, now let's get started." After I had built up some momentum by journaling free hand, I switched to journaling in a separate word processing document and added each new journal entry to the beginning of the document.

This worked for a while, and then I found that I could begin productive writing by journaling for just a few sentences in my dissertation document. I would search for my placeholder, get to the place where I needed to write, review my notes, and read through the last few paragraphs I had written the day before. I would start by writing "What do I want to say today?" or "Okay, what do I want to say here?" Then I would delete these few sentences before I began my writing. As you can see, the process of journaling evolved for me over the course of writing my dissertation. I found that as I built up momentum, confidence, and writing skill, I could rely on increasingly less intensive interventions. Try out the technique of journaling and see how it works for you. Then, as with all techniques I suggest, alter it to suit your needs.

Sometimes, procrastination can really stall you. In these cases, a more intensive intervention is needed. Graduate students, even those who are introverted, can talk through their topics quite adequately but get tied up when they try to put their thoughts into the written word. When one of my students is really struggling with procrastination, I meet with her weekly. I ask her to bring her long outline, and we talk about the next section on the outline on which she needs to work. I pose a set of questions to her and take notes on her responses. By the end of the session, I have written phrases and sentences in the student's own words that can help her get started writing. I often write these notes in an outline format that mirrors her long outline. At the end of our meeting, I make a copy of these notes for me and hand the original notes to the student. I ask her to estimate how much she expects to write by the following week, and we both record it on our notes.

I ask students the following basic set of questions that is general enough to apply to various topics and different sections of the dissertation. These questions walk students through the process of identifying a focus statement and then expanding on that focus statement for the chapter or section:

- What is the important part of this chapter/section?
- What do you want to say about this chapter/section?
- What evidence do you have to back up your point?
- How is this chapter/section going to set up your next chapter/section?

What I find is that students can readily respond to these questions with little hesitation. They just get hung up when they have to translate their thoughts into prose. Remember, you do not have to take on an erudite voice to write your dissertation. Write in your own voice, the voice you use when you talk about your dissertation and respond to the preceding questions. So when you are writing and feel like you are beginning to get stuck, speak aloud as you type. If need be, talk into a digital tape recorder, and then type while playing back the recording. The point is to leverage your strong verbal skills and not to let writing intimidate you to the point where you stall.

Chances are that your adviser will not be able to meet with you weekly to talk through your dissertation. If you think this technique would work for you, do whatever it takes to find someone who will help you to talk through your dissertation and take notes as you are talking. A classmate, writing partner, or a member of your writing group may be able to help you. You may want to look into these types of supports at your university's Center for Teaching and Learning or Writing Center. Although Writing Centers are traditionally for undergraduate students, if they have the resources to help, use them.

What I have found is that first-generation college students and working-class students in my class often struggle with writing. Meanwhile, they make very strong presentations. They just have not had as much experience writing down their thoughts compared with other students. I have worked with American Indian, African American, Latina, and White working-class students. They have all been the first in their families to go to college. In three distinct cases, these students were at risk for being ABD. In two cases, their advisers did not necessarily understand the struggles they were having with writing or their need to teach a few extra courses to support themselves financially. I saw that there was absolutely no reason for these students to remain ABD. They just needed the writing training that they had not received earlier in their academic careers.

I have also observed that returning students who have forged successful careers can struggle with procrastination while writing. These students are interesting because they have very irregular skill sets; some of their skills are highly developed (for example, presenting or supervising) and others are not (such as writing lengthy reports). Returning students need to learn how to leverage their more developed skills to elevate their writing skills.

The working-class, minority, and returning students in my classes respond well to a talking-out-loud protocol to overcome their writing procrastination. Employing this protocol helps them to realize that they can leverage their oral communication skills to complete their dissertations. They have to realize that writing in their own voice is not only acceptable, it is preferable.

9.3. Impatience

The various types of writer's block are not discrete categories. They tend to overlap. I mentioned earlier that I have struggled with procrastination; also, I have and still struggle with impatience. On the surface, impatience may seem contradictory to not finishing a project. How can rushing to get something done interfere with completing it? Bob Boice explains impatience this way:

> Impatience helps block via a sense of urgency: not enough prewriting gets done (e.g., note taking, reflection, conceptual outlining) to permit the preparation that good writing demands; not enough rewriting or proofing is done to convey the writing in polished, error-free form; not enough writing gets done in comfortable, non-fatiguing fashion.[3]

If you experience impatience, you can use a few strategies to overcome it. As mentioned earlier, writers block when they write before they are ready. If you deal with impatience, it is particularly important for you to complete a long outline with references before you start to write prose. You may think that you can jump in and that you have enough to say about your project, but you will often find that you must completely rewrite what you have written. Take the time to do the necessary prewriting and your chances of overcoming impatience increase dramatically.

I can look at a CV and see whether someone struggles with impatience. If you do, you may have multiple projects started but few finished. You have lots of good ideas and the enthusiasm to work on them all, but you jump in too fast and start writing prose before you are ready. Then you get fed up with that project, have another really good idea, and get working on that idea. Although this process may be fun, it is not productive. Your impatience prevents you from engaging in the tedious prewriting that is necessary for you to fluently write the first draft. Your impatience also keeps you from taking the time to adequately revise any prose that you have managed to write.

Keep your projects under control. Place some constraints upon yourself. For instance, you cannot submit another conference presentation until your dissertation proposal is completed. While having evidence of dissemination is important on your CV, I suggest that you balance these career-progressing tasks with completing your dissertation. You are better off if you have one or two presentations and a completed dissertation then five or six presentations and are ABD. Keep the end in mind. Completing your dissertation will open doors that having multiple conference presentations will never open.

I suggest to impatient types (such as myself) that they rely on the twenty-four-hour rule: Do not agree to any additional tasks or responsibilities, no matter how inviting, without thinking about it for twenty-four hours. For those of you who relate to the experience of being overcommitted, try saying this aloud: "That is a great opportunity; thank you. Can I think about it until tomorrow or the end of the week and get back to you?" Be prepared with this response when you are asked to do something. Change it a little, make it your own. Just be sure not to commit to anything else until you complete your dissertation.

Consider adding breaks into your regular writing routine. We impatient types can write endlessly until our hands cramp and our backs are sore. If you experience this and want to develop into an efficient writer, you must change this practice. Slow down and take regular breaks while you write. Buy yourself a timer that is easy to use; it does not need to have any fancy features. At the beginning of your writing session, set a forty-minute interval for yourself. After forty minutes, take a break to stretch or take three deep and slow breaths. Reach down and give your dog a pat on the head.

With regularly scheduled breaks, you can maintain your momentum longer. The chances of developing repetitive stress syndrome or carpal tunnel syndrome are decreased because you are more attentive to the messages your body sends you. Switch your mouse from one side to the other. Move your chair up or down a little. Use an ergonomic keyboard. These techniques can transform you from a sprinter to a marathoner. Being a sprinter worked in your earlier academic career; you could write a short paper and it was just fine—not your best, but good enough that you made it thus far in graduate school. Now, you must employ techniques that keep you going through the long haul.

If you deal with impatience, perhaps you have multiple disappointments in your past or your expectations are unrealistically high. One of my students struggled with impatience with her writing as well as the speed with which she completed her degree. This highly competent returning student entered the doctoral program at her university with the intent of completing the program in four years. Fine, except she worked a full-time job and wanted to attend her sons' soccer games. She did not finish in four years and instead took a hiatus between the end of her coursework and defending her dissertation proposal. Quite a few times during the writing seminar, she shared her disappointment about not meeting her four-year goal.

In one class, she again expressed her dismay at not completing the program in record time. She said, "I entered this program with a four-year plan—as fast as I could. I saw others go through the program. It was hard for me to accept that I was not further along than I was supposed to be."

I looked straight at her and very gently said, "Can you forgive yourself, put that behind you, and move forward?"

These few simple words made a bigger impact on her than I realized when I said them. She mentioned to me later that she found our exchange very freeing. Unrealistic expectations about completing the doctoral program were holding her back. Similarly, unrealistic expectations about your writing can promote blocking and deter you from engaging in a regular writing routine, which is so important to completing a large and daunting project. As you address your impatience, realize that the writing process is about being mortal, realizing your limitations, forgiving yourself, and moving on.

9.4. Depression and Dysphoria

Another form of writer's block, dysphoria or mild depression, may be hindering you from completing your dissertation. In general, students seem to experience two nadir points while pursuing a doctorate. The first is toward the end of the first semester. As would be expected, graduate courses are often much more challenging than undergraduate courses are. Students who excelled as undergraduates are challenged to a new level of performance. Students who were at the top of their classes as undergraduates are now "average." Many doctoral students talk about dropping out during the finals of their first semester. I was one of them. I will always remember sitting on the couch in my parents' living room and talking with my dad. The conversation went something like this:

"Dad, I'm going to drop out of graduate school."

He put his newspaper down and looked at me. He said, "That's okay. Just finish out this semester and then update your résumé. You'll be able to get a job in accounting."

Silence. I had gone back to graduate school as a career change. I had an undergraduate degree in accounting and after a few years working in that field, I realized that I would never be happy spending my working life as an accountant or an auditor. When I conducted interviews with first-year graduate students for my dissertation, I realized that many of them considered dropping out toward the end of their first semester, too. They were studying for finals and finishing papers that challenged them far more than they had been challenged previously.

I finished my first semester and considered my options over winter break. I did not update my résumé but went back to school the following semester. I made a very good decision. Although I still use my accounting skills to create budgets for grant proposals, I am very glad to spend my time writing and teaching instead of reconciling accounts or auditing records.

The second nadir is right before the dissertation. The camaraderie of courses is minimal. The structure provided by coursework is gone. The only thing to pursue is a long-term project. Too often during this time students experience isolation. This is especially true for students who are working on a self-identified project, not a project in line with the adviser's program of research. This is a prime time for depression to creep in and for dysphoria to impede progress on the dissertation. Social support is of great importance during these times. If you have not already recruited a writing group or a writing partner, do it now. If you have not signed up for the dissertation writing seminar offered in your department, do it now. The interpersonal connections, sharing of struggles, and mutual support combat the feelings of depression and dysphoria that you might experience at the beginning of the dissertation phase.

I initiated my own social support network when I was finishing my dissertation. I was in graduate school at a time when formal writing seminars were uncommon. So I asked three other students to join me in a weekly writing group. Each session around my breakfast table, one of us would share her work for half an hour. This person would e-mail her work to the rest of the group earlier so that we could look through it and provide explicit feedback. Afterward, we shared our progress from the week and our graphs. All of us completed our dissertations in a timely manner.

Many times, social support can deter or pull you out of depression or dysphoria, but not all of the time. If depression or dysphoria becomes a hindrance to you, seek the professional support you need. Graduate school is stressful, as is working on a dissertation project and contemplating life after graduate school. If you want to find a therapist, you can go to the university counseling center or obtain a recommendation from your primary care physician or other advanced graduate students. If you are considered an employee of the university based on your teaching or research responsibilities, you can use the Employee Assistance Program for support. If you need professional help, please get the support that you need.

In addition, you may want to consider hiring a writing coach. Although the price for such services may seem exorbitant now, you will realize later that it was a good investment. A writing coach is different from a copy editor. A copy editor fixes your grammatical errors and typos and usually charges less than a writing coach does. A writing coach helps you set long- and short-term goals, improve your writing habits, assess your progress, and prevent writer's block. She probably will copy edit some of your work, but more important, she identifies trends that you can work on as you write. Perhaps you need to work on introductions or transitions or to improve the organization within your chapters. If you hire a writing coach, be sure that she has a track record of writing rather than just being a life coach. Although the services such professionals offer overlap, only another writer can understand the peculiar aspects of the writing process.

Since graduate school, I have managed to keep my writer's block under control. I still rate high on impatience: I have more writing ideas and more one-page outlines in my head than I could possibly write in a lifetime, but I hold myself to a strict rule of finishing one article before starting a new one. I have learned how to turn my weaknesses into strengths and to help others turn their weaknesses into strengths.

You can address writer's block by keeping your writing in perspective. Employ the necessary prewriting tasks, keep important resources handy, rely on your writing partners, engage in a regular writing routine, and seek professional help if necessary. One of the most powerful ways to overcome writer's block is to talk about it with others. For this reason, I emphasize the importance of working on your dissertation with the support of a writing group. Be honest with your writing group. Depending on your relationship with your dissertation adviser, you may not want to expose your writing struggles to her, but you certainly should with your classmates and with the professor who facilitates the writing seminar.

My students find my writing seminar very helpful mostly because I am candid about my past and present struggles with writing. I share the creative ways I can procrastinate and rationalize not working on my writing. I tell my students that if I can overcome my writer's block, so can they. Soon, they too feel comfortable disclosing their writing struggles. We help each other by talking about our struggles and the techniques we use to overcome them so that we can meet our writing goals.

9.5. Group Exercises for Overcoming Writer's Block

If you facilitate or lead the writing seminar or group, please do not feel that you need to hold yourself up as an expert. As mentioned, my students appreciate it when I share my writing challenges with them. I am sure that your students would feel the same way. If you participate in a writing seminar, be sure that your facilitator or professor understands that you are interested in hearing her candid disclosures of her writing successes and failures and what she did to overcome her weaknesses. Let her know that your reason is not to learn about her career challenges, but to foster an open atmosphere where all the members of the writing seminar can support one another.

One semester I shared a blank graph for two months straight. I cringed every time I had to hold up my empty graph. I would say, "I know this is my second month of a blank graph," and the students would tilt their heads a little. They did not remember that I had been on a writing hiatus. They did not ruminate on my blank writing graph between class meetings. They had better things to think about, like their own dissertations and their own lives. I tell you this story to illustrate that we do not hold up our graphs for others; we hold them up for ourselves. The important part of this exercise is not viewing others' graphs but monitoring our own.

Continue to share your graph with your writing seminar or group. Talk about the times when you were able to engage in a regular writing routine and times when you were not. What was going on? What made the difference? Do you hold some beliefs that hinder you from making progress on your dissertation? If so, use the techniques presented in this book to change those beliefs.

By monitoring your work, you can find out what works for you, and then capitalize on your strengths. Some students find out that they write better in the morning; others write for an hour or two after they arrive home. I prefer to write in the morning. At one time I was so rigid about this rule that if I did not write in the morning, I believed I had lost my opportunity to write for that day. My internal critic would say, "You blew it," or "You will never be able to write regularly in the mornings again." I am glad to say that I have since shaken that false belief. Examine your own beliefs and rules. Embrace those that work for you and change those that do not.

After a few weeks, and often when students have been engaged in prose for a while, I have them add one last thing to their long outlines. Next to the chapter titles, I ask them to estimate the percentage of the chapter that is completed. This estimate helps them manage their writing times and gives them a sense of accomplishment. This measure also helps me coach them on which sections they need to spend time on and which sections they do not. If a section is 90 percent finished and another is 15 percent finished, I want them to spend time on the 15 percent section. One perfect chapter does not make for a completed dissertation. As they review the percentages and see which chapters are almost completed, my students envision their progress, which motivates them to continue writing.

Use every tool and technique you can while writing your dissertation. Share them with your dissertation group or writing seminar. Try the strategies that have worked for others. Use your writing graph, long outline, and the support of your writing partners to overcome writer's block and to develop and sustain a regular writing routine.

Notes

1. In *Professors as Writers,* Robert Boice lists seven different forms of writer's block: work apprehension, procrastination, writing apprehension, dysphoria, impatience, perfectionism, and rules (pp. 146–49). I discuss the forms that I find most common among dissertation writers.

2. Anne Lamott, *Bird by Bird,* 21.

3. Boice, *How Writers Journey to Comfort and Fluency,* 148.

10

THE ROLE OF REVISION

I wish there were an easier, softer way, a shortcut, but this is the nature of most good writing: that you find out things as you go along.

—Anne Lamott, *Bird by Bird*

Y our dissertation is the longest and most complex piece of writing you have worked on to date, unless you have published a book or are working on your second doctorate. (If the first: Congratulations! If the second: Call me, we need to talk.) I, too, wish there was an easier, softer way, but the truth is that, as you work on your dissertation, you learn and think differently about your topic, so you have to revise. But that is the point, isn't it? For you to engage in original research, learn something new, think differently about your topic, and contribute to the conversation.

If you can work through the stages of the Single System and engage in a regular writing routine, you will have the luxury of revision. Donald Murray values revision so much that he wrote a whole book on it: *The Craft of Revision*. I find that those who struggle greatly and succeed are the most devoted to a cause. I am that way. Apparently so is Murray. He struggled with revision and once held to the belief that polished prose came flowing out of the pen. If polished prose did come flowing out of the pen (or keyboard) and he was willing to share this secret, I would not have written this book. Instead, he had to modify his beliefs on polished prose and the role of revision. He writes about how his view of revision changed:

> Before, the first draft was that terrible combination of ambition and terror. I wanted to write the great story, article, poem, the one that had never been written before, the one that would establish a new standard for perfection.
>
> And having set that impossible goal, I suffered—appropriately—fear raised to terror, anxiety multiplied by apprehension. But once I got something down, forced by deadline and hunger, I was not suspended between absolute perfection and total failure. I had a draft I could read and develop; I could roll up my sleeves and get to work. . . . It is not admission of failure when you have to rewrite and edit. It is a normal part of the process of making meaning with language. Revision is not punishment, but an opportunity.[1]

I agree with Murray on the importance of revision. Only when I addressed my writing blocks and engaged in a regular writing routine did I have the time for revision. From that point on in my writing career, I began to view revision as an opportunity. I had the time to write a first draft and then had plenty of time to revise, a chance that I did not have earlier because I completed writing projects in a last-minute flurry of activity.

In planning this chapter, I asked students what they thought about revision. Most responded that they had learned about revision through trial and error. Many had not given a lot of thought to revision, but just did it. Few had been taught how to revise. I also asked them what they wanted to learn about revision. They wanted to learn the practicalities of revision. For instance, when you are sitting at your computer and have your butt glued to the chair, what does revision look like? What do you do first? What do you do next? Is there a method that is most efficient for academic writing? Is there a final stage in revision that fluent authors complete? In this chapter, I address the practicalities of revision.

There are two different types of revision: revision at the organizational level, and revision at the content level. Let's start with revision at the organizational level.

10.1. Revision at the Organizational Level

Regardless of how carefully or thoughtfully you develop your long outline before you write your first draft, you still must revise at the organizational level because through the process of writing prose, you find out new information and insights as you go along. You learn more about your topic, you gain a different perspective, and you have to change how you organize your dissertation.

You can rely on the computer-generated table of contents for revision at the organizational level. Think of the various chapters and sections as modules that you can move around like jigsaw puzzle pieces. To revise at the organizational level, print out a copy of your computer-generated table of contents, which serves as your long outline; include only the first two heading levels in this printout so that you can see chapter and section titles. Review the outline. Review the order of the sections carefully. On paper, play around with moving sections. Use a pen or pencil to make changes. Do not rush this step. If you do not jot down some preliminary changes that you discard later, you are not giving yourself enough room to be creative and to review how you think about your topic. You will see that there is no one right way to organize your dissertation; rather, you can emphasize different aspects of your topic by changing the organization of chapters and sections.

Of course, you do not have complete flexibility in the way you order your chapters and sections. Some topics naturally precede others, and your field probably has principles that dictate the organization of dissertations. If you are writing a data analytic dissertation, the order of the chapters is predetermined, and your time revising at the organizational level focuses on the literature review and the conclusions chapters. Likewise, for a journal article dissertation, at the organizational level you revise the literature review and conclusions in the first and last chapters and within each of your manuscripts. For a thematic dissertation, you have the most flexibility in terms of organizing; you can revise at the organizational level among chapters and within chapters.

After you play around with the outline, ask a classmate or two to read through your latest version. Ask them to write notes on the printout. Then spend some time talking them through the outline—you might just discover a few cognitive leaps. Cognitive leaps occur when you leave out important logical steps while you write your dissertation, but manage to supply them while you think and talk about your topic. When you first start your dissertation project, you probably logically think through from A to B to C to D. As you become increasingly expert in your topic, you may jump straight from A to D, a cognitive leap. And if you do, you probably leave out the important steps B and C in your writing.

Whereas you can leap over logical steps while thinking about your topic, you cannot while writing about it. Your audience does not know your dissertation topic as well as you do. Dissertation writers can rarely identify when they make a cognitive leap; they need outside help. By talking through your long outline, you can verbally include the linkages that you have left out on the page. As you talk, your classmates can take notes and jot down those linkages so that you can fill them in later.

Soliciting feedback from classmates and colleagues is essential for identifying flaws in organization. A good friend of mine read an early draft of this book; as a result I reorganized the chapters completely. As I mentioned earlier, I began writing this book for my writing seminar. Not surprisingly, I organized the book as I had organized my class. Students take my class at various times in their doctoral program; some take it in the last semester of their second year of coursework, others after they have defended their dissertation proposal. Because the students are at various stages, we jump among topics that address prewriting, writing fluency, revision, managing dissertation advisers, and writer's block. After reading the early draft of this book, my colleague suggested that I start with the prewriting chapters, followed by the writing chapters, and finish with the revision chapter. I know, I know, that seems so obvious, but I needed a friend to point it out.

To use as an example, I created a figure showing the before and after organization of *Demystifying Dissertation Writing*. I shared the figure with the students in my class and after a brief silence one of my students said, "You know, I thought the same thing." I looked around the beige-painted seminar room and all the rest of the students were nodding their heads in agreement. Everyone could see it but me.

Figure 10.1, Example of Revision at the Organizational Level, is the figure I handed out to my class. I coded the chapters: The chapters that address prewriting are not shaded; the rest of the chapters are. After I coded the chapters, I reorganized the chapters so that all the prewriting chapters came first and the writing and rewriting chapters followed. Although I completely reorganized the book, I did not completely rewrite the book. I combined two chapters from before the reorganization (that

Before	After
1: Overview: The Single System for Academic Writing	1: The Single System for Academic Writing
2: Entering the Conversation	2: Choosing a Topic and an Adviser
3: Making a Contribution	3: Interactive Reading and Note Taking
4: Developing a Regular Writing Routine	4: Citeable Notes
5: Overcoming Writer's Block	5: Focusing on Focus Statements
6: Interactive Reading	6: Transforming a Focus Statement Into a One-Page Outline
7: Interactive Notes	7: Long Outline With References
8: Citeable Notes	8: Developing a Regular Writing Routine
9: Focusing on Focus Statements	9: Overcoming Writer's Block
10. One-Page Outline and Long Outline	10: The Role of Revision
11. The Importance of Revision	
12. A Good Dissertation Is a Done Dissertation	

FIGURE 10.1. Example of Revision at the Organizational Level

is, chapter 2: Entering the Conversation, and chapter 3: Making a Contribution) into one chapter (chapter 2: Choosing a Topic and an Adviser). In another instance, I split what had been a long chapter (chapter 10: One-Page Outlines and Long Outlines) into two chapters (chapter 6: Transforming a Focus Statement Into a One-Page Outline, and chapter 7: Long Outline With References). Had I approached this reorganization by focusing on the 250-plus-page manuscript, the task would have been daunting. Instead, I reorganized a twelve-item list into a ten-item list, which was a very manageable task.

By revising at the organizational level, you can assess the organization of your dissertation without concern for paragraph order or sentence structure. Solicit feedback from your classmates and your adviser on the organizational structure separate from the content. Fold in their feedback. Review your changes, and then later spend your time revising at the content level (described subsequently in this chapter).

After you are satisfied with the reorganization, cut and paste the actual chapters and sections into their new locations so that your document mirrors the hand-written modified version of the table of contents. Then print out a new computer-generated table of contents and place it on the stand next to your computer monitor or tack it on your corkboard.

10.2. Revision at the Content Level

Please leave yourself plenty of time—or as much time as you can—to revise at the content level. The quality of your research and the intellectual inventiveness you use to present a new or revised idea have a large impact on the quality of your dissertation. But so, too, does the quality of your writing and manner in which you package and present your ideas, results, and conclusions. Revising at the content level includes two primary steps. The first step is previewing, smoothing, and reviewing each section. The second step is engaging in targeted and end-stage revision.

Previewing, Smoothing, and Reviewing

For most of the techniques in this book, I suggest that you begin at the beginning and go through to the end. However, when you revise content, I suggest instead that you go through one section at a time, reviewing and revising it until you are satisfied before you go on to the next section.

When you are ready to revise at the content level, pick one section of your dissertation. I recommend that you identify no more than five pages of text to review. Print out the section using a two-page layout so that you can view two pages of manuscript on one page. Not only does this use less paper, it helps you see more of the text at one time. Then read through the whole section. No matter how tempting it is to start marking up the printouts as you are reading, resist this temptation. Read the entire section to remind yourself of the content. Think about the main point of this section. Does the section heading reflect the main point? If not, then revise the section heading.

Next, reread the first paragraph and determine whether the paragraph previews what you present in the section. You preview to provide the big picture to your readers: you paint the picture of the forest so that when you present more details, explanations, and descriptions later, they can see the trees. In the early stages of previewing, feel free to use phrases like "In this section, I present the first, second, and third ideas." Then, while revising, replace the numbering with alternative ways to suggest order by using terms such as *next, following, also,* and *in addition.*

Note the various ideas you preview in this first paragraph and code each idea with a different colored highlighter or use some type of system to differentiate ideas. No need for this to be perfect or too detailed. The reason you code the separate ideas is so that you can ensure that your preview paragraph aligns with the order in which you present those ideas.

I just read a dissertation in which the student wrote in a preview paragraph that she was going to address the impact of excessive alcohol usage on (a) the students who are engaging in excessive drinking, (b) the university or college community, (c) the other students, and (d) the surrounding community. Then, in the section that followed, she proceeded to address the impact of excessive alcohol usage, but using a different order: (a) the university, (b) the classmates, (c) the students, and (d) the surrounding community. I suggested that she begin at the center of the circle with the student and work outward, thereby addressing issues pertaining to (a) the student, (b) the classmates, (c) the university, and (d) the surrounding community and that the preview paragraph align with the subsequent presentation of the text. In this example, you can see that the preview paragraph should align with the ideas presented in the section. Unfortunately, it is rarely that obvious in our own work. As this example shows, we often have a hard time so clearly diagnosing our own work, so we must rely on writing partners and groups to diagnose for us.

After you revise and code your preview paragraph, code the rest of the section. Please resist coding each paragraph as one idea; chances are you have a few ideas that span several paragraphs, which is okay; the goal of the early draft is just to get the words down on the page. Then cut and paste until you have one point per paragraph. Reread the section again, this time on the screen, and mentally code the ideas and continue to revise by cutting and pasting. Most likely, you have to repeat this process a few times until you have one point per paragraph.

I call this process *smoothing*. By using this technique, you smooth out your writing so that it flows in an orderly and organized manner. In an early draft, one idea may span three separate paragraphs. When you are finished revising for content, there should be only one idea, or point, per paragraph. Figure 10.2 shows three ideas represented by three different letters. The left column illustrates an early draft where several points are

Before	Smoothing Process	After
Aaaaaaaaaaaa aaaa. Aaaaaaaa Aaaa.Aaaaaaaaaa. Bbbbbbbbbbbbbbbbbb bbb. *Aaaaaaaaaa aaaa.* Bbbbbbbbbb bbbb. <u>*Cccccccccc cccccccc .*</u> *Aaaa aaaaaaaaaaaaaaaaa* Bbbbbbbbbbbb bbbbbbbbb. Bbbbb. *Aaaaaaaaaaaaaaaa* Bbbbbbbbbbbbbbb. Bbbbbbbbbbbbbbbbbbb b. <u>*Cccccccccccccc .*</u> Bbbbbbbbbbbb bbbbbbbbb. Bbbbb bbbbbbbbbbbbbbBb bbbbbbbbbb. <u>*Ccc ccc cccccccccccccc .*</u> <u>*Cccccccccccccccccc .*</u> <u>*Cccccccccccccccc*</u>	*Aaaaaaaaaaaa aaaa. Aaaaaaa aaaaaaaaaaaaaaaaa.* Bbbbbbbbbbbbbbbbbb bbb. *Aaaaaaaaa aaaaaa.* Bbbbbb bbbbbbbb. *Aaaa aaaaaaaaaaaaaaaa Aaaaaaaaaaaaaaaa* Bbbbbbbbbbbb bbbbbb. Bbbbb bbbbbbbbbb. Bbbbbb bbbbbbbbbbbbb. <u>*Ccc ccccc cccc .*</u> Bbbbbb bbbbbbbbbbbbbbbb. Bbbbbbbbbbbbbbbbbbb b. <u>*Cccccccccccc cccccc .*</u> Bbbbb bbbbbbbbbbb. <u>*Ccc ccccccccccc cccc.*</u> <u>*Cccccccccccccccc .*</u> <u>*Cccccccccccccccc .*</u>	*Aaaaaaaaaaaa aaaa. Aaaaaaaa aaaaaaaaaaaaaaaa. Aaaaaaaaaaaaaaaa. Aaaaaaaaaaaaaaaaaaaa aaa. Aaaaaaaa aaaaaaa.* Bbbbbbbbbbbb bbbbbb. Bbbbb bbbbbbbbbbbbbbb. Bbbbbbbbb. bbbbbbbbbbbbb Bbbbbbbbbbbbbbbb Bbbbbbbbbbbbbbbb. Bbbbbbbbbbbbbbbbbbbb bbbb. <u>*Cccccccccccc cccccc .*</u> <u>*Cccc cccccccccccccccc .*</u> <u>*Ccccccccc .*</u> <u>*Cccc cc cccccccccccccc .*</u> <u>*Cccccccccccccccc ..*</u>

FIGURE 10.2. Smoothing to Get One Point per Paragraph

included in and across various paragraphs. The middle column shows an intermediary step that starts to smooth out the ideas. You usually cannot complete smoothing in one step, although I would love for you to prove me wrong. The right-hand column represents a section after revision at the content level where each paragraph includes one point.

After you smooth a section, double-check to make sure that your preview paragraph still aligns with the order of the points presented in that section. Then determine whether you need a review paragraph. In many cases, a review paragraph is not necessary. Review sentences or paragraphs are useful when you switch among ideas or when you present complex and intertwined ideas.

When you have finished smoothing your paragraphs, you can directly address issues of sentence structure and grammar. I address this issue just so that you do not think I forgot the importance of cleaning up sentence structure and correcting grammatical errors. I didn't. Nonetheless, chances are you were doing this during the smoothing process as you were reading, reviewing, and rereading your work.

When you are satisfied with the smoothing of this section, move to another section and repeat the smoothing process. If you try to smooth at the chapter level, you might find the process to be much less efficient because you must read the whole chapter a few times and continually remind yourself of the details and examples in it. Plus, you have already revised at the organizational level for the chapter. As long as the text below the section headings aligns with the section headings, the chapter will be organizationally sound.

Revising for content at the section level provides you with an ongoing sense of accomplishment. After you have revised a section, check it off on the table of contents that is displayed on your desk. As you spend time revising at the content level, you might be surprised at what you can accomplish by focusing on one section at a time.

Revising for organization and content are two tasks that should, and do, take up a considerable amount of time. Just as you engaged in a regular writing routine while writing your first draft, likewise use the same time management tasks to sustain your writing routine through the long revision stage. You might find that after you revise for organization and then for content, you go back and revise for organization again.

Targeted Revision

After you have revised for organization and content, are you ready to distribute your dissertation? No. The final aspects of revision are crucial. Targeted revision addresses your particular writing idiosyncrasies. End-stage revision ensures that you do not distribute a dissertation manuscript that has a glaring grammatical error in the first paragraph or on the first page.

As part of targeted revision, search your manuscript for over-usage of your favorite phrases. One of the last things that I do when I revise is to search for a few key terms. I tend to start sentences with phrases such as *That is* or *This is* all too regularly. A very kind and supportive reviewer of one of my book chapters pointed out this idiosyncrasy. (I suspect that this reviewer is an English professor, but I will never know.) As part of my targeted revision, I search for these two phrases and replace them, switching the sentence from the passive voice to the active voice. For example:

Before: There are a few points I want to highlight.
After: I highlight a few points.

Another of my writing idiosyncrasies is overuse of the word *yet* at the beginning of sentences. Tim Prevo, a recent college graduate who helped me edit this book, pointed out this idiosyncrasy. Toward the end of any writing project, I now conduct a search for *yet* and replace most instances with a different word or phrase. A final idiosyncrasy I report here is that I regularly write *and also* in my early drafts. I do not worry about it then because I know what I am saying and it helps me to keep my momentum going while I am writing. But I know that using these two words side by side is redundant. As part of my targeted revision, I search for *and also* and delete one of the words. To wrap up, I search for the word *blank* to make sure that I replaced this placeholder with a more appropriate word or term.

I want to emphasize that I needed feedback from colleagues to revise the organization of my book. I also needed feedback from my colleagues to identify some of my writing idiosyncrasies. Starting every other sentence with *yet* seemed quite fine to me until others pointed this out.

It can be difficult to revise your own writing. Writing researchers John Hayes and Linda Flower conclude, "Writers have difficulty detecting faults in their own text."[2] They reviewed research on young and adult writers and found that when people have prior knowledge of the text (as you do when you revise your own writing), they detect far fewer problems than when they do not have prior knowledge. Apparently, while reading our own work, we fill in unclear explanations and mentally correct usage. Not only do we need writing partners and groups to keep ourselves accountable, apparently we also need them to point out the problems in our writing that we cannot identify on our own.

End-Stage Editing

End-stage editing is when you ensure that you submit a piece that is neat, organized, and free of typographical errors. First impressions have an undue influence on how your committee members assess your whole dissertation. As I work on my own writing, I continue to be amazed at how many times I can revise a sentence and overlook that I typed *work* when I wanted to type *word*, or when my brain translates the *your* down on the page into *you* up in my brain. I know of only two ways to address this. The first is by bribing, paying, or bartering with others to read your work. As supported by the research of Hayes and Flower, I can spot obvious typos in my students' and colleagues' writing and they can spot them in mine.

The other way to address this problem is to read your work aloud from the computer screen or printed page. Sit down, block out a few hours of non-high-productivity time and read your dissertation aloud. If I may be so presumptuous, I do not blame you if you think, "Are you nuts?!?!? Read my whole dissertation aloud?!?!" Very valid point; just read through the abstract and as much of the first chapter as you can. Then, read through the last half of the final chapter. Now, don't get me wrong. Reading aloud only the first section is not license for getting sloppy afterward; just use your time wisely as you read your dissertation aloud.

If the first few pages are really messy, some advisers do not continue reading through the whole dissertation but return it with the dictate that you spend more time polishing the project before you distribute it again. You want the first part to be very clean. If your adviser and committee members get through the first few pages without being distracted by typos or grammatical errors, they naturally look for these errors less and focus more energy on the content of your dissertation.

In most instances, I suggest that you revise section by section. Only for the abstract do I suggest that you revise at the sentence level because the abstract is the most concentrated part of your dissertation and provides your committee members with a cognitive map of the ideas you present later. Within each paragraph, move from the general to the specific or from the specific to the general. Make sure each sentence in the abstract contains only one point. In your abstract, briefly describe what you did for your dissertation research, why it is important, and highlight the most important results or conclusions.

For your final read-through (not aloud this time), I recommend that you begin at the beginning and go through to the end. Try to do this in as few sittings as possible so that you notice when you repeat yourself in different chapters or sections. Make sure that your introduction adequately previews the rest of the dissertation. Check that the numbering of your pictures, figures, graphs, and other illustrations matches the number you use in text. And, finally, read through your dissertation from beginning to end to revel in your accomplishment. What you are reading represents years of preparation and focused attention. As much as possible turn off your internal critic, fix only minor typographical or grammatical errors (except when a section really needs additional revision), and enjoy reading your work.

10.3. Group Exercises for Revision

Give yourself plenty of time for revision. You may want to share your revision task with a friend. Exchange manuscripts, perhaps one chapter at a time. Revising someone else's dissertation is much less anxiety provoking than is revising your own. Also, editing others' work is one of the best ways to improve your own writing because you are exposed to other terms, techniques, and writing styles. Plus, you see that others, like you, do not write perfect prose the first time.

When you solicit or give feedback on a manuscript, keep a few points in mind. The first and perhaps most important rule is to give the type of constructive feedback that you would want from others. In addition, make it easy for others to provide you with the feedback you need by making explicit what you want from them, and vice versa. Do you want feedback that focuses on the content and does not focus on typos? Or do you want feedback on typos, word usage, and grammatical structure? Let your reviewers know by typing those criteria on the first page of your document before you send it to them. That way, they do not have to remember your requests in the e-mail message and can review your requests each time they open your document.

When I provide feedback to my students, I make comments throughout their drafts. I provide feedback that I would want to receive. Rather than writing something like "this section doesn't make sense," I suggest ways for them to address the problem, such as suggesting that they rewrite the focus statement and then reorganize the main points for that section. At the top of their papers, I also identify two or three global items for them to address. Often I suggest that they write shorter paragraphs and that they do not engage in cognitive leaps. Or I suggest that they work on their transitions and be explicit about the significance of their study. They can focus on changing only one or two aspects of their writing at a time. After they address the earlier suggestions and develop their craft of writing, then I offer a few more suggestions.

What you might take from this chapter is that students, colleagues, reviewers, and friends were all instrumental in the revision process for my writing, in pointing out my particular overuse of words or imprecision of phrases. One theme I stress in this book is the importance of writing partners, colleagues, and friends who can help improve your writing process. By pointing out defects in your writing that you cannot detect, they also help you improve your writing product.

Like Donald Murray, many writers, including me, think writing is all about revision. With revision, you can finalize a dissertation of which you can be proud. Remember, the goal is not a perfect dissertation. A good dissertation is a done dissertation.

Notes

1. Donald M. Murray, *The Craft of Revision*, 3, 143.
2. John R. Hayes and Linda S. Flower, "Writing Research and the Writer," 1110.

EPILOGUE AND ENJOYING THE JOURNEY

Success comes from within.

—Ralph Waldo Emerson

MY MOTHER WAS VISITING ME and for some reason we were in my office. I am sure she was helping me in some way, but now I cannot recall. My back was turned toward her as I filed some papers in my filing cabinet.

"Did you ever think you would be here?" she asked. As I turned around, I saw that she was sitting at my desk and looking around at the diplomas on the wall.

"No, not in a million years," I replied. We talked, reminisced, and chuckled a little bit about my journey, remembering the times when she would stop by while I toiled away at my dissertation to see whether I wanted to go shopping. Or when my best friend and her family held up a three-by-seven-foot sign that read "Yeah, Dr. Peg" at my graduation and kept it up until I saw it, despite the grumblings from those sitting behind them.

If you have never questioned whether you could finish your dissertation project and earn a doctoral degree, I hope that this book makes your journey a little easier. Perhaps by using the Single System and learning from others, your writing process becomes more efficient and the journey becomes more enjoyable.

On the other hand, if you do question your ability to earn your doctorate, I hope the Single System makes the journey not only easier, but also possible. Here, you have read about others' struggles and successes. You have learned about and perhaps tried some techniques that you can use to complete your dissertation. I hope these techniques are useful wherever your journey leads you after you graduate.

While I was finalizing this book, I stayed with a friend who was working in Atlanta. We visited the Dr. Martin Luther King Jr. memorial where I came across this quote by Dr. King: "I can never be what I ought to be until you are what you ought to be, and you can never be what you ought to be until I am what I ought to be."

Writing this book brought me one step closer to who I ought to be. Through this process, which started the day I met Bob Boice, I have turned my weakness into a strength.

I hope finishing your dissertation brings you one step closer to who you ought to be. I hope everyone who reads this book benefits. Use it as an inspiration by rereading some of the struggles and successes captured between the covers. Use it as a reference to remind yourself of the Single System writing techniques. I wish you increased efficiency, much happiness, and an enhanced capacity to enjoy the journey.

APPENDIX A
ELEMENTS OF HUMANITIES RESEARCH

T HIS JOURNAL ARTICLE published in *American Historical Review* provides an example of the various elements of academic writing.[1] I use an article rather than a book simply for space considerations. Although this article does not represent the variability that exists within the humanities fields, please use it as an example from which you can identify the various elements of research and then apply them to the formats and standards in your field. The article is inherently interesting to me because my father took the sea journey from Ireland to the United States, albeit, under much more favorable conditions.

For this example, I scanned six pages of the article, not including footnotes. I realize that this format makes it a bit difficult to read, which is unfortunate because it is a very interesting article. But you want to finish your dissertation and I want to finish this book, so we must work within this constraint. Be that as it may, I added annotations as an example of interactive reading to point out the elements presented in the first few pages of the article.

Tyler Anbinder, the author, sets up his research by presenting the big picture. The big picture, in this case, focuses on the historical context for the research. The author initially highlights the experience of one Irish emigrant and uses this as an example to address issues pertinent to a group of Irish people who emigrated to the United States during the famine years (1840s through the 1850s). The author addresses the big picture by detailing the experiences of Ellen Holland while she was in Ireland, during the voyage, and then when she settled in the Five Points

From Famine to Five Points:
Lord Lansdowne's Irish Tenants Encounter North America's Most Notorious Slum

TYLER ANBINDER

AS NEW YORKER ELLEN HOLLAND looked back over her first forty-seven years of life in 1860, she must have wondered whether she was blessed or cursed. "Nelly" had been born and raised in southwestern Ireland in the County Kerry parish of Kenmare. There she grew up surrounded by jagged mountain peaks and lush green hills that sloped dramatically to the wide, majestic Kenmare River. Nelly and her family were tenants of the marquis of Lansdowne, whose estate was home to 13,000 of the most impoverished residents of nineteenth-century Ireland. Visitors to the huge property commonly chose terms such as "wretched," "miserable," "half naked," and "half fed" to describe the poor farmers and laborers who dominated its population.[1]

Observers invoked such descriptions of Nelly's birthplace even *before* 1845, when a mysterious potato blight began to wreak havoc on the meager food supply. By late 1846, Kenmare residents began to succumb to starvation and malnutrition-related diseases. As conditions continued to deteriorate in early 1847, the death toll multiplied. An Englishman who visited the town of Kenmare at this time wrote that "the sounds of woe and wailing resounded in the streets throughout the night." In the morning, nine corpses were found in the village streets. "The poor people came in from the rural districts" in such numbers, wrote this observer, "it was utterly impossible to meet their most urgent exigencies, and therefore they came in literally *to die*." Tens of thousands fled Ireland in 1847, but almost none of the Lansdowne tenants could afford to emigrate. Relatively few had journeyed from this isolated estate to America in the pre-famine years, so t[...] [...]te from abroad that financed the voyages of ma[...]uge parts of Ireland.[2]

Although an abatement of the potato fung[...]d declare the emergency over, such decrees mea[...]had suffering in Kenmare. Most of Lansdowne's ten[...]one

pound or meal and thirteen[...]nine

days at s[...] compounded the suffering that Holland and her Lansdowne shipmates had already endured at home.[4]

But Nelly was a strong woman, determined to build a better life for her family. Like most of the Lansdowne immigrants, she settled in New York's "Five Points" neighborhood, the most infamously decrepit slum in North America. There, surrounded by drunks, brothels, and other Irish immigrants, and living in one of the most squalid blocks of tenements in the world, Holland and her family set to work rebuilding their lives. After years of unemployment, they must have been eager and delighted to take even the lowly jobs available to them. Her husband Richard found work as a menial day laborer. Ellen became a washerwoman. The boys undoubtedly pitched in as well, for when Ellen opened an account at the Emigrant Savings Bank in September 1853, thirty months after her arrival in New York, she was able to deposit a substantial sum, $110, equivalent to about $2,350 today.[5]

Despite having accrued this significant nest egg in a relatively short period, Holland's struggles continued. By July 1855, both her husband and eldest son were dead. One might have expected her to dip into her savings to help make ends meet during such trying times, but Nelly did no such thing. In fact, despite losing her family's two primary breadwinners, by 1860 she had increased her bank balance to $201.20 (more than $4,200 today), a real feat for a widow who, just eight years earlier, had been on the brink of starvation and had lived the first thirty-eight years of her life in a land of chronic underemployment and hunger. More surprising still, among the hundreds of Lansdowne immigrants who came to New York—most, like Holland, arriving utterly destitute—such relative financial success was not all that unusual.[6]

Hundreds of thousands of men and women like Ellen Holland emigrated from Ireland to North America during the famine years. Yet, dramatic as her story may be, few such tales can be found in the historiography of the famine immigration to America. This has resulted to a large extent from the divided nature of Irish studies.

The Big Picture

The Big Point and Reason for Studying Source

as the best works in the field treat either the Irish or the American story but rarely follow the emigrants from Europe to America. A number of fine books have examined the conditions that drove about 2 million Irishmen to flee the Emerald Isle in the famine years, but these studies do not offer detailed accounts of their subjects' fates in America.[7] The best works on the Irish in the United States likewise devote relatively little attention to Irish Americans' lives before they immigrated. David M. Emmons in *The Butte Irish* and Kevin Kenny in *Making Sense of the Molly Maguires* trace their protagonists to West Cork and West Donegal respectively, but the reader gets little sense of how individual lives changed.[8] Studies of famine-era Irish immigration to Canada and England have followed the same historiographic pattern.[9]

Given the current trend toward "internationalizing" our study of history (both the *American Historical Review* and the *Journal of American History* have recently focused attention on this subject), one might imagine that studies of the Irish diaspora would have begun to compare their subjects' pre- and post-emigration lives more fully. Those who study the seventeenth and eighteenth-century Atlantic World," for example, have produced a number of sophisticated and influential monographs that cross national boundaries, but this trend has had little impact on historians of immigration, the vast majority of whom study the nineteenth and twentieth centuries.[10] Most sociologists, in contrast, have warmly embraced the concept of "transnationalism," arguing that modern means of communications and transportation have created a new breed of immigrant who simultaneously main-

tains strong ties to two lands.[11] Historians, justifiably skeptical about claims that contemporary immigrants are so different from their predecessors, have been reluctant to jump onto the transnational bandwagon. Those interested in immigration and ethnicity have instead focused on issues such as "whiteness" (exemplified by Noel Ignatiev's provocative *How the Irish Became White*), nativism, and other aspects of cultural history.[12] Research on the Irish elsewhere has followed the same trends, although a recent survey of the field in England lamented that "the academic study of the Irish in Britain continues to lag far behind its counterpart in the United States." Even the appearance of a six-book series entitled "The Irish World Wide," while significant, did not portend any sea change in Irish historiography, as virtually every essay in the collection looked at the Irish in a single town or city. The 150th anniversary of the famine did produce a surge in publications on that subject, but little that would help explain whether the relative financial success of Ellen Holland and her friends was typical or exceptional.[13] And there are no signs of a revival in the kinds of "mobility studies," pioneered more than thirty years ago by [...] ght enable us to put the financial achieve- [...] into context.[14]

[...] -American historiography would certainly [...] suppose[...] must be unusual. A deep pessimism has [...] pervade[...] the famine immigrants were a kind of lost generation fated to be victims of disease, nativism, low-paying jobs, and over-crowded tenements in North America or England. Any significant improvement in their circumstances, such studies imply, came in the lives of their assimilated children. There are exceptions, but most scholars continue to believe, as Oscar Handlin put it more than fifty years ago in *Boston's Immigrants*, that the famine

Theoretical Perspective

Original Premise and Reconsidered Premise

Irish were both economically and socially "fated to remain a massive lump in the community, undigested, undigestible."[15]

When I began investigating the history of Five Points, I assumed that the prevailing gloomy picture of the famine-era immigrants would be borne out on its mean streets. Given that Five Points' residents were the most impoverished in antebellum New York, I expected to find them barely scraping by from payday to payday. I was especially sure that the Lansdowne immigrants would fit this stereotype. They made up about one in nine of Five Points' Irish-Catholic inhabitants in the 1850s and were concentrated overwhelmingly in the most squalid tenements in the neighborhood's most decrepit and crime-ridden blocks. But the bank balances of Ellen Holland and her fellow Lansdowne immigrants force us to reconsider such long-held preconceptions.[16]

Elements of Humanities Research

slum in New York City, a slum brought to life in the movie *The Gangs of New York*. Then he uses the example of Holland to examine the political, economic, and social experience of the group of Irish emigrants who traveled the same journey as she did.

The big picture should set up the presentation of the big point, which addresses the questions: "Why should I (the author) care about this research?" and "Why should my audience care?" The big point and the reason for studying a particular source, group, text, or argument are often closely linked, as in this example. The author explains that, although the research on the Irish in Ireland and the Irish in America is plentiful, his research is important because it follows a specific person, or a group, from Ireland to the United States and relates her circumstances from before, during, and after emigration. In addressing the big point, the author lets readers know that he is focusing a new lens on stories that have been told before:

> Hundreds of thousands of men and women like Ellen Holland emigrated from Ireland to North America during the famine years. Yet, dramatic as her story may be, few such tales can be found in the historiography of the famine immigration to America . . . as the best works in the field treat either the Irish or the American story but rarely follow the emigrants from Europe to America.[2]

In the next paragraph, Anbinder introduces the theoretical perspective. He applies an "internationalism" perspective, an approach that has become increasingly popular in studies of other populations but that has not been embraced by historians studying immigration. The author identifies the perspective and defines internationalism by stating, "Given the current trend toward 'internationalizing' our study of history . . . one might imagine that studies of the Irish diaspora would have begun to compare their subjects' pre- and post-emigration lives more fully."[3]

Before presenting his research, the author states his original premise and how his research will encourage his audience to reconsider this premise. The reconsideration is based on his access to and analysis of newly released primary sources, namely, bank records from the Emigrant Savings Bank where Ellen Holland deposited her savings:

> When I began investigating the history of Five Points, I assumed that the prevailing, gloomy picture of the famine-era immigrants would be borne

out on its mean streets. . . . But the bank balances of Ellen Holland and her fellow Lansdowne immigrants force us to reconsider such long-held preconceptions.[4]

Despite the fact that this article is not representative of all humanities research, it provides one example of how academic writing includes fairly well defined and established elements: the big picture, the big point, reasons for choosing sources or samples, the theoretical perspective, the original premise, and the reconsidered premise or conclusions.

Notes

1. *The American Historical Review* by Tyler Anbinder. Copyright 2002 by University of Chicago Press. Reproduced with permission of University of Chicago Press.
2. Tyler Anbinder, "From Famine to Five Points," 353–4.
3. Ibid., 354.
4. Ibid., 356.

APPENDIX B
ELEMENTS OF SOCIAL
SCIENCE RESEARCH

I N THIS EXAMPLE from the social sciences, the journal article takes a positivistic approach toward research, which includes the testing of hypotheses. As you read social science articles or dissertations, you might find it helpful to identify the big picture, the big point, the hypotheses, and the rationale for sample selection. Then you can start to see the patterns commonly used in your field and can fashion your own work to follow. For this example, and based on my interest in the development of writing expertise, I present an article published in the *American Educational Research Journal*.[1] Because of space limitations, I include only the first three pages of the article and I added annotations as an example of interactive reading to point out the elements presented in the first few pages of the introduction.

Please skip over the abstract and focus on the introduction. Notice that the authors provide the big picture: They say that the teaching of writing has been neglected, and they support this contention by referencing a report by a commission established by a well-respected professional organization in education (that is, the College Board). The authors quickly tell why they, and you, should care about this topic and telegraph the big point in the sentence "This is important for two reasons." In the next two sentences, the authors expound on the reasons you should care, and they use writing clues to draw the audience's attention. The authors do not get fancy here. They start the sentence by explaining the first reason with "First" and start the second sentence with "Second":

Improving the Writing, Knowledge, and Motivation of Struggling Young Writers: Effects of Self-Regulated Strategy Development With and Without Peer Support

Karen R. Harris and Steve Graham
Vanderbilt University
Linda H. Mason
Pennsylvania State University

Writing development involves changes that occur in children's strategic behavior, knowledge, and motivation. The authors examined the effectiveness of self-regulated strategy development (SRSD), a strategy instructional model designed to promote development in each of these areas. Instruction focused on planning and writing stories and persuasive essays. The addition of a peer support component to SRSD instruction aimed at facilitating maintenance and generalization effects was also examined. SRSD had a positive impact on the writing performance and knowledge of struggling second-grade writers attending urban schools serving a high percentage of low-income families. In comparison with children in the Writers' Workshop condition, SRSD-instructed students were more knowledgeable about writing and evidenced stronger performance in the two instructed genres (story and persuasive writing) as well as two uninstructed genres (personal narrative and informative writing). Moreover, the peer support component augmented SRSD instruction by enhancing specific aspects of students' performance in both the instructed and uninstructed genres.

KEYWORDS: peer assista[...]evelopment, strategy instruction, struggling le[...]

The Big Picture

In 2002, the National Commission on Writing in America's Schools and Colleges released a report, *The Neglected "R,"* designed to focus national attention on the teaching of writing. This commission was established by the College Board, an organization of more than 4,300 colleges, and created in large part because of growing concern that the writing of students in the United States "is not what it should be" (National Commission on Writing, 2003, p. 7). This concern is well founded given results from the National Assessment of Educational Progress (NAEP) indicating that three of every four

Harris et al.

students in the 4th, 8th, and 12th grades demonstrate only partial mastery of the writing skills and knowledge needed at their respective grade level (Greenwald, Persky, Ambell, & Mazzeo, 1999). Furthermore, almost one in every five first-year college students require a remedial writing class, and more than one half of new college students are unable to write a paper relatively free of errors (Intersegmental Committee of the Academic Senates, 2002).

The commission's report highlights the need to make writing improvement a national goal. A critical element in developing an effective and comprehensive writing policy is the identification of effective instructional procedures, not only at the secondary level (where the report concentrates most of its attention) but with younger students as well, especially primary grade children who experience difficulty learning to write. This is important for two reasons. First, providing effective writing instruction to these children from the start should help ameliorate their writing problems (Graham & Harris, 2002). Second, waiting until later grades to address literacy problems that have their origin in the primary grades has not been particularly successful (Slavin, Madden, & Karweit, 1989).

The development and validation of effective writing procedures must also

The Big Point

The development and validation of effective writing procedures must also focus on how to improve the writing performance of children in poor urban settings. Although the NAEP writing scores of children served in these schools, including poor students as well as Black and Hispanic students, improved from 1998 to 2002, the gap between each of these groups and White and Asian students remained substantial (Persky, Daane, & Jin, 2003).

One purpose of the current study, therefore, was to examine the effectiveness of an instructional program in improving the performance of young, struggling writers attending urban schools serving a high percentage of children from low-income families. A struggling writer was defined as a child who scored at or below the 25th percentile on a norm-referenced test of writing performance that measured the inclusion of specific thematic elements in a story and who was also identified as a poor writer by the classroom teacher. The experimental intervention, self-regulated strategy development (SRSD; Harris & Graham, 1996, 1999), is compatible with current theories on the

Self-Regulated Strategy Development and Young Writer

development of competence in a subject-matter domain (Alexander, 1992, 1997; Chi, 1987; Harris & Alexander, 1998; Pintrich & Schunk, 1996). These conceptualizations emphasize that learning is a complex process that depends, in large part, on changes that occur in a learner's strategic knowledge, domain-specific knowledge, and motivation (Alexander, Graham, & Harris, 1996). Although the primary focus of SRSD is on teaching students strategies fo

Although the primary focus of SRSD is on teaching students strategies for successfully completing an academic task, students are also taught knowledge and self-regulatory procedures (e.g., goal setting, self-monitoring, and self-instruction) needed to carry out the target strategies and better understand the task. In addition, instructional procedures for fostering aspects of motivation, such as student effort, are embedded within the model. This emphasis on addressing multiple aspects of development reflects a basic premise that guided construction of the SRSD model over 20 years ago (Harris & Graham, 1999). students who experience academic difficulties benefit from an integrated approach to intervention that directly focuses on cognitive, metacognitive, behavioral, and affective factors. The theoretical underpinnings of this emphasis included Meichenbaum's (1977) integration of cognitive and behavioral perspectives; Brown and Campione's research (Brown, Campione, & Day, 1981) on the development of self-regulation, metacognition, and critical components of strategy instruction; and the work of Soviet theorists, such as Vygotsky (1978), on the origins of self-control.

Previous investigations have shown that SRSD has a strong impact on improving the writing performance of upper-elementary and middle school students (effect sizes typically exceed 0.80, including enhancing the writing of youngsters attending urban schools (Graham & Harris, 2003, in press). The effectiveness of SRSD with primary-grade students, however, has been tested in only one study with third-grade children (Graham, Harris, & Mason, 2005), and data are limited on the effects of the model on writers' knowledge and motivation. In the study involving third-grade students, SRSD instruction in how to plan and write stories and persuasive essays had a strong impact on the writing performance of children who were experiencing difficulty learning to write. After treatment, SRSD-instructed students' stories and persuasive papers were longer, more complete, and qualitatively better than papers written by control students (effect sizes exceeded 1.78 for all of these measures). Positive effects of SRSD instruction were also observed in an uninstructed genre, informative writing (the effect size for quality was 1.08), and students' knowledge about writing was boosted as well. In the present study, we extended research on SRSD and writing by assessing the impact of this instructional approach on the writing, knowledge, and motivation of even younger struggling writers (second graders) who attended urban schools serving a high percentage of children from low-income families.

Hypothesis #1

Rationale for the Sample

Intervention/ Treatment

Elements of Social Science Research

First, providing effective writing instruction to these children from the start should help ameliorate their writing problems. Second, waiting until later grades to address literacy problems that have their origin in the primary grades has not been particularly successful.[2]

Very early in the article, in the first sentence of the fourth paragraph, the authors state the first hypothesis for this study. Once again, they make it very easy for you to follow their logic and argument. To introduce the first hypothesis, they write: "One purpose of the current study, therefore, was to examine the effectiveness of an instruction program in improving the performance of young struggling writers attending urban schools serving a high percentage of children from low-income families."[3]

Next, they introduce the intervention by writing, "The experimental intervention, self-regulated strategic development (SRSD) is compatible with current theories on the development of competence in subject-matter domain."[4] Then they explain how this intervention is positioned within the theoretical framework of learning.

Soon afterward, they provide their reasons for identifying the sample they chose to research. To explain the rationale for sample selection, the authors first explain the current limitations in the literature by stating that the intervention had only "been tested in one study with third-grade children, and data are limited on the effects of the model on writer's knowledge and motivation." The authors demonstrate how their research adds something new to the field when they state: "In the present study, we extended research on SRSD and writing by assessing the impact . . . on the writing . . . of even younger children (second graders)."[5]

For what it is worth, I will point out what interests me about this article. First, the intervention basically teaches young students how to "develop and organize ideas for writing a paper." This is prewriting. These authors are teaching second-grade students how to engage in prewriting, and the data show that young children exhibit stronger writing performance as a result. Second, in one intervention group, the students learned about prewriting in a peer support setting. The young students shared what worked for them and what did not, and they helped each other to apply what they were learning to other subjects. The students in the intervention group with peer support showed even greater improvements, albeit on a more limited range of writing outcomes. While I contend that prewriting and writing groups are important for dissertation writers, the authors of this article have found that these are also beneficial for young writers.

Notes

1. *American Educational Research Journal* by Karen R. Harris, Steve Graham, and Linda H. Mason. Copyright © 2006 by Sage Publications Inc. Journals. Reproduced with permission of Sage Publications Inc. Journals in the format Tradebook via Copyright Clearance Center.

2. Karen R. Harris, Steve Graham, and Linda H. Mason, "Improving the Writing, Knowledge, and Motivation of Struggling Young Writers," 296.

3. Ibid., 296.

4. Ibid., 296–7.

5. Ibid., 297.

BIBLIOGRAPHY

American Historical Association. "Statement on Standards of Professional Conduct." American Historical Association, 2005. www.historians.org/PUBS/Free/ProfessionalStandards.cfm (accessed January 28, 2008).

Amrein, Audrey L., and David C. Berliner. "The Effects of High-Stakes Testing on Student Motivation and Learning." *Educational Leadership* 60, no. 5 (2003): 32–38.

Anbinder, Tyler. "From Famine to Five Points: Lord Lansdowne's Irish Tenants Encounter North America's Most Notorious Slum." *American Historical Review* 107, no. 2 (2002): 351–87.

Behar, Ruth. *Translated Woman: Crossing the Border with Esperanza's Story*. Boston: Beacon Press, 1993.

Boice, Robert. *How Writers Journey to Comfort and Fluency: A Psychological Adventure*. Westport, CT: Praeger, 1994.

———. *Professors as Writers: A Self-Help Guide to Productive Writing*. Stillwater, OK: New Forums Press, 1990.

Bower, Bruce. "Road to Eureka!" *Science News*, March 22, 2008, 184–85.

Boyle, Peg. "The Socialization Experiences of New Graduate Students." PhD diss., State University of New York at Stony Brook, 1996.

Brians, Paul. *Common Errors in English Usage*. Wilsonville, OR: William, James & Co., 2003.

Carlson, Neil R., C. Donald Heth, Harold Miller, John W. Donahoe, William Buskist, and G. Neil Martin. *Psychology: The Science of Behavior*. 6th ed. Boston: Pearson, 2007.

Carroll, Lewis. *Alice's Adventures in Wonderland*. New York: Heritage Press, 1941.

Covey, Stephen R. *The 7 Habits of Highly Effective People*. New York: Simon & Schuster, 1989.

Ericsson, K. Anders, and Neil Charness. "Expert Performance: Its Structure and Acquisition." *American Psychologist* 49, no. 8 (1994): 725–47.

Fleron, J., P. Humpke, L. Lefton, T. Lindquester, and M. Murray. "Keeping Your Research Alive." Paper presented at the Project NExt Program. Minneapolis, MN, Jan. 9, 1995. Quoted in Richard M. Reis, *Tomorrow's Professor: Preparing for Academic Careers in Science and Engineering.* New York: IEEE Press, 1997.

Franzoi, Stephen L. *Social Psychology.* 4th ed. Boston: McGraw-Hill, 2006.

Germano, William. *From Dissertation to Book.* Chicago: University of Chicago Press, 2005.

Goldberg, Bonni. *Beyond the Words.* New York: Tarcher/Putman, 2002.

Granovetter, Mark S. "The Strength of Weak Ties." *American Journal of Sociology* 78, no. 6 (1973): 1360–80.

Gravois, John. "In Humanities, 10 Years May Not Be Enough to Get a Ph.D." *Chronicle of Higher Education,* July 27, 2007, A1, A9–10.

Hallowell, Edward M. "Overloaded Circuits: Why Smart People Underperform." *Harvard Business Review,* January 2005, 1–9.

Harris, Karen R., Steve Graham, and Linda H. Mason. "Improving the Writing, Knowledge, and Motivation of Struggling Young Writers: Effects of Self-Regulated Strategy Development With and Without Peer Support (PDF)." *American Educational Research Journal* 43, no. 2 (2006): 295–340.

Hayes, John R., and Linda S. Flower. "Writing Research and the Writer." *American Psychologist* 41, no. 10 (1986): 1106–13.

Hyland, Ken. *Writing in the Academy: Reputation, Education and Knowledge.* London: Institute of Education, University of London, 2007.

Jacks, Penelope, Daryl E. Chubin, Alan L. Porter, and Terry Connolly. "The ABCs of ABDs: A Study of Incomplete Doctorates." *Improving College and University Teaching* 31, no. 2 (1983): 74–81.

Jackson, H. J. *Romantic Readers: The Evidence of Marginalia.* New Haven, CT: Yale University Press, 2005.

Jaschik, Scott. "Why and When Ph.D. Students Finish." *Inside Higher Education,* July 17, 2007. www.insidehighered.com/news/2007/07/17/phd.

King, Stephen. *On Writing: A Memoir of the Craft.* New York: Pocket Books, 2000.

Kuhn, Thomas S. *The Structure of Scientific Revolution.* 2nd ed. Chicago: University of Chicago Press, 1962/1970.

Lamott, Anne. *Bird by Bird: Some Instructions on Writing and Life.* New York: Anchor Books, 1994.

Litt, Jill S., Andrea Wismann, Beth Resnick, Rebecca Smullin Dawson, Mary Hano, and Thomas A. Burke. "Advancing Health and Environmental Disease Tracking: A 5-Year Follow-up Study." *American Journal of Public Health* 97, no. 3 (2007): 456–63.

Lovitts, Barbara E. *Making the Implicit Explicit: Creating Performance Expectations for the Dissertation.* Sterling, VA: Stylus Publishing, 2007.

MLA Handbook for Writers of Research Papers. 7th ed. New York: Modern Language Association of America, 2009.

Murray, Donald M. *The Craft of Revision.* New York: Harcourt Brace Jovanovich, 1991.

Nash, Robert J. "Facing One Another in This Place: Using Moral Conversation to Talk About Controversial Topics in College Settings." *Journal of College and Character* IX, no. 4 (2008): 1–9. www.collegevalues.org/pdfs/Nash.pdf (accessed May 7, 2008).

———. "How September 11, 2001 Transformed My Course on Religious Pluralism, Spirituality, and Education." *Religion and Education* 29, no. 1 (2002): 1–22. http://uni.edu/coe/jrae/New_Folder/Nash_Sept.11.pdf (accessed June 6, 2009).

———. *Liberating Scholarly Writing: The Power of Personal Narrative.* New York: Teachers College Press, 2004.

National Center for Education Statistics. "Table 229. Employees in Degree-Granting Institutions, by Race/Ethnicity and Residency Status, Sex, Employment Status, Control and Type of Institution, and Primary Occupation: Fall 2005." Digest of Education Statistics 2006. Washington, DC: US Department of Education, Institute of Education Sciences. http://nces.ed.gov/programs/digest/d06/tables/dt06_229.asp?referrer=list (accessed January 11, 2008).

Picciano, Joseph, Elizabeth Rudd, Emory Morrison, and Maresi Nerad. "CIRGE Spotlight on Doctoral Education #3: Does Time-to-Degree Matter?" 2008. Seattle: Center for Innovation and Research in Graduate Education, University of Washington. http://depts.washington.edu/cirgeweb/c/wp-content/uploads/2009/02/t2degree_12-31-08c.pdf.

Publication Manual for the American Psychological Association. 5th ed. Washington, DC: American Psychological Association, 2001.

Sternberg, Robert J., Lynn Okagaki, and Alice S. Jackson. "Practical Intelligence for Success in School." *Educational Leadership* 42 (1990): 35–39.

Strunk, William, Jr., and E. B. White. *The Elements of Style,* 3rd ed. New York: MacMillan, 1979.

Turner, A. L., and T. R. Berry. "Counseling Center Contributions to Student Retention and Graduation: A Longitudinal Assessment." *Journal of College Student Development* 4, no. 6 (2000): 627–36.

Webster's New World College Dictionary. 2nd ed. Ed. by David B. Guralnik. New York: Williams Collins, 1979.

Wikipedia contributors. "Comparison of Reference Management Software."

Wikipedia, The Free Encyclopedia. http://en.wikipedia.org/wiki/Comparison_of_reference_management_software (accessed January 19, 2009).

———. "Copyright Infringement." *Wikipedia, The Free Encyclopedia.* http://en.wikipedia.org/w/index.php?title = Copyright_infringement&oldid = 243396005 (accessed October 9, 2008).

———. "Plagiarism." *Wikipedia, The Free Encyclopedia.* http://en.wikipedia.org/w/index.php?title = Plagiarism&oldid = 244023107 (accessed October 9, 2008).

Wilson, S. B., T. W. Mason, and M. J. M. Ewing. "Evaluating the Impact of Receiving University-Based Counseling Services on Student Retention." *Journal of Counseling Psychology* 44, no. 3 (1997): 316–20.

Wulf, William A. "Diversity in Engineering." *The Bridge* 28, no. 4 (1998): 8–13.

INDEX

Also available from Stylus

What They Didn't Teach You in Graduate School
199 Helpful Hints for Success in Your Academic Career
Paul Gray and David E. Drew
Illustrated by Matthew Henry Hall
Forewords by Laurie Richlin and Steadman Upham

"In just under 150 pages the authors, of course, do not get deeply into any subject, but they hit the mark so many times and in such an entertaining and succinct way that readers will feel well informed when they finish. This book will be a welcome and valuable addition to the bookshelves of all graduate students and new faculty. We plan to buy one of these for each of our incoming faculty and doctoral students."—**Dennis E. Gregory,** *The Review of Higher Education*

Teaching Your First College Class
A Practical Guide for New Faculty and Graduate Student Instructors
Carolyn Lieberg

"An indispensable tool to anyone embarking on the task, both graduate instructors and newly-appointed assistant professors. Lieberg dispenses some graceful wisdom on the art of teaching without being overly prescriptive or reducing classroom strategies to easy formulas. Whether you are new to the classroom or a veteran who is mentoring first-time teachers, you will find that this book provides a sensible blend of pedagogical history, practical advice, and pointed anecdotes aimed at helping new teachers spend less time being fearful and more time becoming successful." —**Nancy K. Barry,** *Assistant to the Dean for Advising and Academic Support, Luther College*

Barbara E. Lovitts & Ellen L. Wert
Developing Quality Dissertations in the Humanities
Developing Quality Dissertations in the Sciences
Developing Quality Dissertations in the Social Sciences

"These booklets are a terrific resource for graduate students who want to learn what faculty members look for in a quality dissertation. They will also prove useful to faculty as they convey explicit expectations to their students about a quality dissertation."—**Karen L. Klomparens,** *Dean and Associate Provost for Graduate Education, Michigan State University*

"These booklets are a useful tool for demystifying the culminating element of doctoral studies—the dissertation. I recommend that students use them to initiate conversations with their advisors about how to achieve high quality dissertations."—**Chris M. Golde,** *Associate Vice Provost for Graduate Education, Stanford University*

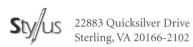 22883 Quicksilver Drive
Sterling, VA 20166-2102

Subscribe to our e-mail alerts: www.Styluspub.com